More praise for *Honey, Do You Need a Ride?*

"Jennifer Graham is the hilarious, pee-your-pants running partner you wish you had. She'll make you want to move to Boston just to pound out a few miles alongside her and slam down a ginormous hot-fudge sundae with her post-run. If you love running, laughing, eating, and reading in equal measure, you'll love this book."
—Eileen Button, author of *The Waiting Place: Learning to Appreciate Life's Little Delays*

"Attention fat people of the world: Jennifer Graham is so wise and funny in *Honey, Do You Need a Ride?* that you might just find yourself lacing up your sneakers and following her around the track. She is lovable and hilarious as a gazelle trapped in the body of a fat girl."
—Debra Galant, author of *Rattled* and *Fear and Yoga in New Jersey*

"*Honey, Do You Need a Ride?* is a humorous journey shared proudly by its author. Just as Jennifer Graham's chosen form of recreation keeps her mentally and physically fit, reading Jennifer's story is equally therapeutic—even motivational—to the reader. Jennifer proves there is a runner in all of us! From her first-person perspective, she shows that running is a sport for life."
—Joann Flaminio, first female president of the Boston Athletic Association, organizer of the Boston Marathon

Honey, Do You Need a Ride?

Confessions
of a
FAT
Runner

JENNIFER GRAHAM

BREAKAWAY BOOKS
HALCOTTSVILLE, NEW YORK
2012

ISBN: 978-891369-80-3
Library of Congress Control Number: 2012942679

Published by Breakaway Books
P.O. Box 24
Halcottsville, NY 12438
www.breakawaybooks.com

FIRST EDITION

Contents

For David Knight,
who gave me my voice.

Author's Note

In the interest of privacy, two names were changed.

Not Jo-Jo's or Foggy's.

PART ONE

"I have not failed. I've just found 10,000 ways that won't work."
—Thomas Edison

one

The Shadow Yells Walrus

The problem with being a fat runner is this: Everyone wants to give you a ride.

Nobody's ever around when you have a flat tire or run out of gas on a lonely stretch of road, but try to go out for a leisurely three miles after dinner, and suddenly there's a Samaritan with a cell phone behind every shrub.

"You okay, honey? Ya need a ride? Is there somebody I can call?"

And don't even think about sprinting between telephone poles, or they'll be calling 911.

"Po-lice? I just saw a fat lady running down Front Street! Somebody must have stolen her purse!"

The unwelcome ministrations of strangers are only the start of my troubles. Of course, there's my lumpy old body.

People say I have nice hands, and my shoulders are kind of pretty when I remember to stand up straight, but nobody's looking at them when I run. Not even me. Usually I'm staring straight ahead, trying to avoid eye contact with the shadow that precedes me by a couple of steps. If the sun is high, my shadow doesn't look so much like me as it does the Stay-Puft Marshmallow Man. Panting. Truly, it's a terrifying sight.

Don't get me wrong. I love to run. I'm good at it, and I can go on forever. The spirit cries "gazelle." But the shadow yells "walrus." It blows me up by at least twenty pounds.

And don't even get me started on the topic of my thighs. You skinny people, you have no idea what a gift it is to move around without your inner thighs rubbing together like a couple of superglued hams. Since childhood, I've had a major case of Thigh Rub, which sounds like a fried-chicken seasoning, but is just another hidden indignity of the chronically overweight.

I can tell exactly how much I weigh, on any given morning, by how intimate my inner thighs are with each other. The five pounds I keep losing and gaining back, that's where they live and multiply, although they do occasionally head north to visit their time-share in my upper arms.

You would think anyone who runs as much as I do would have legs like my mother's: thin and shapely, with polite thighs that aren't always groping each other. But my mother's legs are wasted, as far as I'm concerned, because she has never run with them. Running, I believe, is a leg's highest purpose.

My legs are not so beautiful, but they are sturdy and effective. I like this quote that's on my bulletin board: "Darling, the legs aren't so beautiful. I just know what to do with them." That was Marlene Dietrich, the late German actress. I don't know much about her except that her director wanted her to lose weight.

Well, running wouldn't have helped her. I have been running for twenty years now, and I'm still a card-carrying endomorph. I have this soft and thick body that looks like it was stuffed to order at Build-A-Bear. All I'm missing are the tiny aviator glasses and a zipper down my back.

I figure I've run more than ten thousand miles. This defies all laws of science because, despite the calories expended, despite the muscle strands lengthened, the calluses thickened, and the ibuprofen consumed, my body does not look significantly different from back when I didn't run. It's hard to believe that these thick thighs, slapping together rhythmically like a slow metronome, basically carried me from my home in New England to the West Coast and back, two times. Dammit, shouldn't I look like a twig?

But if the science doesn't work, the math does. Ten miles a week, fifty-two weeks a year—with time off for four miserable pregnancies —equals 10,400 miles. And most weeks, I run more than ten miles.

Not that I'm bragging. Ten miles is nothing for those haughty, long-legged ectomorphs—I call them Shirtless Wonders—who routinely cover that distance on their lunch breaks. The running magazines to which I subscribe regularly deflate my ego with headlines like "How to Run a Successful 10K on Only 20 Miles a Week!"

Only?

When I run twenty miles in a week, I get out the party hats and confetti.

No matter. Dr. Kenneth Cooper, the fitness guru who coined the word *aerobics,* says if you run more than fifteen miles a week, you're running for something other than fitness. Ten miles a week is great. But without a significant reduction in ice cream (a joy-killing sacrifice I refuse to make), they won't make you thin. So for now, I remain a fat runner. There are worse things to be. Sedentary, for example, or agnostic.

I am neither, I'm proud to say. This week, I have done these things:

Rollerbladed. Ridden a horse. Ran twelve miles. Swam (albeit miserably) in a cold lake. Ridden my bike twenty-five miles at Cape Cod, including two glorious miles alongside the ocean, where I paused to watch a seal playing in the surf. I did all these things, fat.

I also have prayed, for guidance and for strength. Not that I'm not already strong.

Because, while being a runner makes you strong, being a *fat* runner makes you stronger.

For one thing, you're exercising carrying built-in weights. Skinny people have to go to Target to buy those cute little five-pound weights they carry along when they work out. Mine are free. When I run, I am Rocky Balboa training on the snowy hills of Russia with a log on his shoulders; the load I carry is sweet-and-sour chicken many years congealed. But God is good, so surely the training effect is the same. I've often thought that if I were to magically drop fifty pounds, I could not only finish but win a marathon, propelled by the superhuman strength of my long-suffering legs.

But there's more. Beyond physical strength, being a fat runner makes you mentally tough. You learn to handle everyday indignities that would emotionally slay most everybody else. Take, for example, the time I went to a spa and requested the "Runner's Revenge" massage that was the treatment of the day.

That devil-witch masseuse looked at me skeptically and then had the nerve to ask, "Why?"

"Uh, because I *run?*" I said crossly, thinking of the new, fun ways I'd be spending her tip.

But when the hour was up and my deep tissues throbbed contentedly, I forgave the ignorant rube. After all, how was she to know?

Most runners are ectomorphs, emaciated and square-jawed. Me, I'm soft and round. God made me this way.

Well, God, and vanilla ice cream.

Lord knows, I've tried to change my shape. I've been either on a diet, or starting one tomorrow, every day since I turned twelve. When I started running regularly, I truly believed that, after a lifetime of pudgery, at last I was going to be enviably slim. I bought a green silk dress three sizes too small and hung it in my closet for inspiration. Running, I just knew, was going to put that dress on me, zip it loosely up my back.

Twenty years later, it's still hanging in my closet, unworn. That infernal zipper has never gone more than half the way up.

But I keep running anyway, and along the way, I have acquired a coach. You may have heard of him: He was this rock-star Olympian, Steve Prefontaine. Yeah, I know he's been dead thirty-seven years; it's a minor metaphysical challenge. But look, after eighteen years of marriage, I am single and trapped a thousand miles from home, with four children, two donkeys, and a really bad attitude. Dead coaches are the least of my worries.

I need a new body and a new attitude. I seek to find them at a South Carolina resort.

Ten years ago, when I lived in Charleston, the Holy City on the South Carolina coast, I ran the Kiawah Island Half-Marathon as a lark. I had, at that time, never run more than six miles at one time, and I just wanted to see if I could finish. (I did.)

This year, I've decided to run it again, to see if a dead guy can coach, and if I've achieved anything at all over the past few decades, or if I've just been wasting time, running in place.

My husband—my *former* husband—used to say to me, "Honey-bunny, those voices in your head, they're not real." Maybe he's right. Who knows what compels the eternal narration that goes on in our brains? Some believe God is whispering to us; well, God, or Satan. For others, it's nothing more than conscience: wholly human, wholly us. Or maybe inner dialogues are simple intuition, slyly donning a familiar, trusted diction and tone.

There's a name for them, interior locutions, and while they're commonly associated with crazy people, some not-so-crazy people have freely confessed to them. Charles Dickens used to have conversations with his literary characters, conversations that were so real to him, he would laugh out loud in church. Mother Teresa, Joan of Arc, William Blake, Mahatma Gandhi, the German composer Schumann—all conversed delightedly with passing visitors in their heads.

Are they real, our inner voices? Or, as Scrooge said to Marley, are they "an undigested bit of beef"?

The angel perching on one shoulder is the foil to the devil sitting on the other, and of course they're not real, material things—not like, say, the note my husband wrote me a few years ago that says, "You're stuck with me; I will never, ever leave you."

But today I woke up, and the husband who will never, ever leave is not here. His closet is bewilderingly empty. But the infernal little angel and devil are still around. Who's to say what is real and what is not? For now, I'm thinking that reality is highly overrated, and sometimes, it's the voices in our heads that convey life's deepest and most reliable truths.

To hell with reality. As the cocktail napkin says, it's a nice place to visit, but I wouldn't want to live there.

Still, my race is a couple of weeks away. Reality may yet come for me on the hill at the end of Mile 10.

Meanwhile, I guess I should explain why I use the f-word. You know the f-word I'm talking about: *fat.*

It took me a lot of years to get to a place where I could say or write it without cringing. What a god-awful syllable that is. Even as insults change with new generations, the power of that nasty word remains.

When my seven-year-old daughter came home crying because a classmate had called her fat, all I could do was hug her. I knew. Been there, felt that. I wanted to take a baseball bat to the offending kid's head.

In our house, we have an unwritten list of bad words, which no adult or child is allowed to utter. There are two f-words. *Fat* is one of them. (Yeah, I know; it's a wild life we lead, right on the edge of propriety.)

Why then, does Mom get to call herself a fat runner?

Well, it's because I love words but hate euphemisms. Plus-sized? Give me a break. I am fat. Really, I am. (Though I still blush a little when I have to say it.) Every morning, my high-tech torture device, previously known as a scale, gleefully calculates my body-fat percentage and, cackling, pronounces mine "high," even if I ran four miles effortlessly the previous day.

Now, it's true that parts of me are more fat than others. (See "Thighs and Middle Back, J. Graham.") And sometimes, I wear it well. One doesn't live multiple decades on this planet without learning how to competently disguise one's jiggles.

It is also true that I am fatter at different times of the year. I am much more fat in January, after the eggnog season, than I am in June, while trying on swimsuits at Macy's after two months of halfhearted Atkins. Depending on how much I am running, how stressed I have been, and how close I live to a Dairy Queen with a drive-through, I wear anywhere from a size 12 to size 20. Up and down the ladder I go.

But, January or June, Target 12 or Lane Bryant 20, I'm still fat, in multiple places. If you need someone to say "bless you" and hand you an adipose tissue, I'm your gal.

Don't misunderstand; I'm not *proud* of this. God love them, I am never going to join the National Association to Advance Fat Acceptance. I wish all people—me included—were varieties of thin. We'd be healthier. We'd live longer. On this, the science is solid.

But the reasons people remain fat are secret and complex, and only vaguely related to calories. One person may be overweight because of an overbearing mother; another because of an underperforming thyroid; another (ahem) because she likes soft-serve ice cream too much. But, to the enduring gratitude of the American diet industry, few of us fat people ever accept it. Most of us keep longing to be thin.

I do, although my reasons for this have changed over the years.

When I was younger, I wanted to be thin, first to stop the teasing, and then to have a boyfriend, and eventually a fiancé. After the wedding and the first child, I wanted to lose the baby fat, which turned into toddler fat, which turned into teenager fat. (My fat is amazing like this; like a magician, it performs tricks!)

But I'm not motivated by those things anymore. It's ironic. I started to run because I wanted to be thin. Now I wish I were thin because I run.

Sometimes, in the cereal aisle at the grocery store, or in the parking lot at Target, I see people I can instantly identify as runners. Everything about them screams *athlete*—their posture, their shoes, their calves. They look like my tribe. I can tell they spend their free time like I do.

I try to catch their eyes, looking for that flash of connection we all crave, that moment when you think, *Here is a person who knows my experience. Here is a person who gets it.* But their eyes hardly ever meet mine. In this body, they don't recognize *me*. I don't look like a runner, probably not even a walker. I look like someone who eats a cholesterol-laden dinner every night and then flops on the couch. (Not that there's anything wrong with that; I hear it's wonderful, but as a single mom of four, I can only imagine.)

Sometimes I wonder why I still care, why I can't just resign myself to this body. I am ridiculously healthy, after all; even my doctor says so. My blood pressure is excellent, and my resting pulse rate is in the fifties. (Take that, all you Shirtless Wonders.)

But there are still scads of other reasons I would like to be thin, many of them that don't have anything to do with my former husband's wispy girlfriend.

For instance, I have never, in my whole life, had a stomach that didn't protrude. I am curious just to see what abs are like. Just for a day.

I would like to climb on the scale at the doctor's office without feeling an urgent need to remove my shoes.

And I would like to show my two daughters that weight does not have to control their lives, that the opposite is true: that all their lives, *they* can control their weight.

But most of all, since I love to run so much, what I really want is to *look* like a runner. I want to go to a race expo and hang with the human gazelles and look like someone who could actually keep up with them.

But I don't, and I can't. Not this week, anyway.

For now, calling myself a fat runner is simply truth telling. And yeah, it's also an etymological middle finger to everyone whoever called me—or my daughter—fat.

People, especially writers, love to talk about how much words matter. They boast that the random arrangement of vowels and consonants is the pinnacle of human achievement.

People who say that don't know how to construct bridges, or make a really good crème brûlée.

Actions mean more. Words are just words. And all of us control the levers that give words authority. Use a word yourself, devoid of its cruel connotations, and over time it becomes benign. You strip it of its power to jeer.

But that's a point of personal privilege. Anyone else who calls me fat goes to bed an hour early and has to clean stalls for a week.

two

The Construction of Fort Dimples

I suppose I should explain about the divorce, and the donkeys, and I promise I'll get to all that. The donkeys add a surreal dimension to my life unattainable by dogs and cats. I can't tell you how many cards I've gotten over the years that tell me what a fine ass I have. Believe me, this is a compliment I would never, ever get if I didn't have Jo-Jo and Foggy.

You're gonna love them; everyone does. Once, we entered Jo-Jo in Weston Nurseries' Halloween costume contest for pets, and she won the grand prize. Of course she did. Those poor dogs and cats in their Dracula and Superman costumes never had a chance; even their owners were gushing over Jo-Jo. You've never seen anything so cute as a four-hundred-pound donkey dressed up like a ballerina, her white belly hanging over the tutu. She was alarmingly reminiscent of, well, me.

I, too, have a belly that hangs over the tutu, and I've had it most all of my life. Me and my fat, we go way back. But don't take my word for it. There's evidence: a picture of me as a toddler, standing in a sandbox in my backyard, with chipmunk cheeks and dimpled arms, and puffy little thighs already in serious need of liposuction. I was two.

Looking at this picture, I want to blame my mother for my weight. I can just see her holding the camera and beaming at me proudly, going, "Isn't she just the cutest thing?"

Cute, like a white donkey in a tutu.

But it's not fair to blame my mother. I'm an adult now, and the responsibility for my body is all mine. The past is past. Bygones are bygone. Heck, I have my own children now.

So I blame my grandmother.

Gram was a co-conspirator in my development because of my parents' divorce. My mother and I lived with her and my grandfather until I was twelve. And you never really understand your childhood until you, too, grow up and procreate, and then get to watch the women who raised you interact with *your* kids. Believe me, it's a revelation.

I would take my infant son over to visit, and my grandmother would fuss over him, repeatedly saying "He looks hon-gry!" mere moments after he'd nursed.

Explains a lot.

Observing this, I developed new sympathy for my thighs, which apparently were force-fed liters of Similac long past the point of satiation. Alas, once those fighter fat cells were established, they pledged to defend Fort Dimples for life, and they've done a heck of a job. If I could get them a contract with the US armed forces, we'd have been out of Afghanistan a long time ago.

My weight went up and down throughout childhood, but in truth mostly up. If I lost two pounds, the fighter fat cells would go to war and triumphantly bring back three. The only time I came close to a normal-for-my-height weight was when I was nine. My mother was in graduate school at Appalachian State University, and we lived in an efficiency apartment for a few months in Boone, North Carolina. Since my mom wasn't working, we had no money. For months, we subsisted on Vienna sausages and frozen fish sticks. I lost eight pounds that summer, but it's a diet I can't recommend.

And of course, as soon as we moved back to my grandparents' home, where country-fried steak and pot roast were dinnertime staples, the pounds returned, accompanied by friends.

I looked hon-gry.

My mother tried, she really did, even though she couldn't comprehend my struggle. Sally, always thin, had been Miss Bennettsville High School and had done some modeling in college. She didn't understand my heft, or the reasons for it, any more than I did.

On paper, weight loss seems so simple. One pound equals thirty-five hundred calories; expend thirty-five hundred calories, lose a pound. What's so difficult about that?

Beats me, and twelve and a half million overweight American kids.

But my mother didn't give up. She took me to doctors and to Weight Watchers, signed me up for swim camp and tennis lessons, and offered valuable cash prizes if I would lose ten or twenty or fifty pounds. Nothing worked.

For one miserable semester, she insisted I play on a girls' basketball team, and I ran up and down the court at Cardinal Newman High School (well, whenever they let me off the bench) without sinking a basket or losing a pound.

Basketball wasn't the only sport I tried. I rode horses. And I took tennis lessons. I never got good enough to play on a team, but I could occasionally hit the ball with moderate proficiency. When I was twelve, my mother moved us to an apartment complex that had a couple of courts. After school, I would go to the court alone and whack balls against the backboard until I sweated off a pound.

I was particularly diligent at this on Weight Watchers' weigh-in day.

The pounds came off; they went back on. "She looks hon-gry!" the defenders of Fort Dimples would say, and I'd be off to the refrigerator to forage for leftovers: rice and chicken gravy, hamburger-and-potato casserole, homemade buttermilk biscuits. My mother is a very good cook. (When I first got my own apartment, she gave me a copy of *The Joy of Cooking* with the recipe for apple pie marked.)

It also didn't help that I was a latchkey kid. With no one home when I got home from school, I was free to pillage and consume without disapproving eyes.

I ate too much even as I grew older, and the barbs of my peers grew sharper each year. I was called fatso, a whale, a white elephant.

Once, when I had a sunburn in high school, a friend (a *friend*!) called me "an overgrown tomato."

Another time, I was doing cannonballs into my apartment complex's swimming pool, and a kid splayed across a lounge chair hollered "Thar she blows" each time I jumped in.

Then there was the time I went into a convenience store to pick up a bottle of Coca-Cola for my mother. (The sugary kind; Diet Coke wasn't released until I was in college.) The cashier smirked and said to me, "Do you know how many calories are in that?"

I was twelve years old.

Really, couldn't we instate the death penalty for anyone who makes fun of a fat child?

High school was no better. I had few dates, all with boys who attended other schools. The relationships didn't last long. I was never anyone's steady, was never invited to a prom. My eight-year-old stepbrother, visiting one weekend, made me cry at the dinner table one night when he innocently offered that perhaps if I would lose some weight, I would have more dates.

He was right, of course.

I ate and dieted, dieted and ate. I lost no weight, but I muddled through by embracing the traditional interests of nerds. I was a good student, and I became editor of the student newspaper and president of the eight-member Latin Club. I was in the Bible Club, sang in the folk choir at my church. At a Christian coffeehouse, I met and briefly dated a boy I would marry in fourteen years.

Through it all, my weight was always an issue, the awkward canvas on which everything else was painted. I became increasingly self-conscious and sensitive; some said overly so. At my first real job—I was a reporter at a weekly newspaper—the boss's wife called me in one day to tell me I needed to take criticism less personally. Hah. Mrs. Ethridge, thin and beautiful, had never been fat.

You skinny people, you should know this: Fat people are sensitive because we *have* to be—because we are perpetually bruised emotionally by skinny jerks. For the overweight, hypersensitivity is a Darwinian reflex; it enables us to spot and dodge incoming insults.

Well, most of the time.

When I was seventeen and a junior in high school, I had an independent study in leadership, which I now see as proof that the American school system is in an irrevocable state of decline. Somehow I got away with this instead of studying something that might have actually helped me in life, like how to hire a divorce lawyer (hint: choose one you dislike) or how to deworm a donkey who won't open her mouth.

Anyway, the self-directed course was supposed to help me be an effective leader when I became editor of the school newspaper the next year. My adviser was Mrs. Levy, a thin, bespectacled teacher whose main job appeared to be managing the Spring Valley Student Council (aka the Society of Popular, Thin Girls and Jocks). Still, she was nice enough to me, and I was excited to be summoned to her room, where the Student Council hung out, so we could establish my goals.

I lumbered in, wearing my usual outfit: a hooded gray sweatshirt and Levi's with the waist size scratched out. The room was empty, except for Mrs. Levy and one of the Student Councilettes, who was supposed to be doing her homework but, from the look of the tiny hearts doodled in the margin of her spiral notebook, probably was not.

Cindi did not look up. To her kind, the overweight are always invisible.

Mrs. Levy waved me over to her desk and took out a binder, in which she'd scribbled some notes.

"Okay, let's get to work," she said, a little too enthusiastically. "I've got some ideas for the first four weeks, and then we'll meet again and plan for the next."

I nodded.

"First, we're going to work on public speaking," she said. "Things like eye contact. Hand gestures. Enunciation. I want you to write some speeches and deliver them in front of me."

"Okay," I said. "No problem."

I was already comfortable talking to a group. I was comfortable singing in front of a group. Heck, I could have been on the Student Council, too, if I'd been popular enough.

"Then I thought we'd study Robert's Rules of Order. You need to get a copy of that."

I wanted to suggest that the use of similes in Prussian literature would have been more useful to my future life than this. But being the amiable sort, I just nodded.

I glanced over at the highly bored Cindi, who had pulled a brush out and was detangling her hair.

Mrs. Levy continued. "Oh, and Jennifer? There's one more thing I want you to do this semester, as part of this course. I want you to lose some weight."

I froze. Which, amazingly enough, didn't stop my cheeks from turning all hot and blistery.

Cindi suddenly straightened and, for the first time since I'd walked in, looked interested in what was happening my way.

I wanted to crawl under the desk, but I wasn't sure I'd fit.

"Twenty pounds would be good," Mrs. Levy went on, oblivious to my mortification. "But at least ten."

She pushed her glasses on top of her head and looked pointedly at my gray sweatshirt, which was doing its damnedest to conceal my belly, although its damnedest wasn't enough.

"It really does affect what people think of you," she said sweetly.

Oh, I dunno, you moron, you think?

No, I didn't say that at the time. That's me, now. I've got a little bit of an attitude these days.

But back then, all I knew to do was smile and nod. Being gracious in the face of atrocity comes easy to southerners, and the obese.

"Okay, you're right. I know. I'll work on that," I mumbled. At first opportunity, I fled to my locker, where I had a Hershey bar stashed.

That semester, I did not, of course, lose any weight. But I did a really good job avoiding eye contact with Cindi every time I passed her in the hall.

That, in a nutshell, was high school. That was my pre-running life. It wasn't *horrible*. I didn't have to hide in a closet from the Nazis. I didn't lose my legs to polio, or live in an abandoned boxcar in a railroad yard during the Depression, like my grandmother-in-law did.

But, like my life now—maybe like yours?—it was harder than people knew. Harder than it should have been.

Recently, I filled out a questionnaire, and one of the questions was, "Are you an emotional eater?"

I grumbled to myself, "Is there any other kind?"

Except for rare cases of metabolic disorders, most of us who overeat do so to numb or nurture ourselves. So of course, the first thing a fat child does when wounded is run home and eat everything in the pantry.

Two immutable laws: The rich get richer, and the fat get fatter. This is why, despite the plethora of diet plans and diet pills and diet magazines that clamor for our attention and money, many fat people remain fat all their lives. Once wrapped in it, it's hard to claw your way out of the miserable net. Harder still, if you are ensnared as a child. Studies have shown that half of overweight teen girls become severely obese—eighty to one hundred pounds overweight—by the time they turn thirty.

Which is why, at age twenty-five, I was fifty pounds overweight; capable of eating an entire pizza by myself, but unable to jog a quarter mile without stopping.

But here's the thing: I know *thin* people who can't jog a quarter mile without stopping.

Maybe the difference between the people who can and who can't has *nothing* to do with their bodies. Maybe the difference is what's in their dreams.

three

First Steps

So what gets a self-conscious, sedentary, overly sensitive overgrown tomato of a girl to drag herself off the couch and start running around town scantily clad?

It wasn't the nagging of my mother, or a coach, or the demand of an out-of-bounds teacher. It wasn't the flat, tanned stomachs I so admired on the covers of *Cosmopolitan* magazine. It wasn't even that my love life was lacking. It was another damn voice in my head.

This one turned up while I was sleeping. I suppose you might call it a dream.

That's right, I had a dream, just like Martin Luther King Jr., only his was about lofty ideals of mankind, and mine was about me running around a lake.

I was twenty-five and zaftig, and at the time lived alone in a duplex with thin carpet and peeling paint. I was chronically broke and perpetually overdrawn. I drove a beat-up Corvette that broke down more often than it ran. (The license plate said "TOW ME," and no, I'd never been on water skis in my life.) I worked hard at my job, but other than that, things weren't so great. My only exercise consisted of hauling my empty pizza boxes to the trash can. But one night, I dreamed I ran around a lake.

It was a specific lake: Lake Katherine, which sits at the center of the neighborhood where I grew up, in Columbia, South Carolina. (Motto: Two hours from the beach, two hours from the mountains; two hours from everywhere you'd rather be.)

Now, don't go thinking I grew up rich because I lived in a neighborhood with a lake. I was grandfathered in. Literally.

My father left town when I was six months old and my mother was twenty. He left with her car and the vacuum cleaner, which remains a mystery to us both to this day. What would any man want with a vacuum cleaner?

Too embarrassed to even take off her wedding ring, and with no money or child care, my mother packed her clothes and my crib and moved us in with her parents, who had recently purchased a four-bedroom ranch home. My grandmother, who was about to send her last child to college, was happy to postpone her looming empty nest. She would take care of me while my mother finished college, and later while my mother was at work.

The arrangement was hard on my mother, but good for me. Lake Katherine was—and still is—a lovely community. There were children my age on our street, and we lived on a cul-de-sac. I rode my bike with no worries of strangers or traffic. A grown-up was always home; the house was always clean. I waded in the cold creeks that tumbled into the lake, and on weekends my mother and I picnicked on its banks, picking wildflowers and inspecting the turtles sunning themselves.

Two great mysteries of the world: Why would any man steal a vacuum cleaner? And how do turtles know how to line themselves up on rocks in order of size, like little snapping von Trapps? Even with a college education, I can't figure these things out.

Nor can I figure out why I had that dream.

When I had it, it had been thirteen years since I'd lived near Lake Katherine, although my grandmother, by then a widow, still lived there. It was especially odd because I had no experience running at all, except sluggishly on the tennis court. I had no apparent desire for exercise of any kind; I certainly engaged in none.

But there it was, one night as I slept on a cheap water bed: a rapid-eye image of me running around Lake Katherine. It was me, all right—only me strong and quick. And I wasn't even breaking a sweat.

When the alarm clock buzzed, I hit the snooze button and lay there awhile with my eyes closed. In my mind, in the thick haze that separates sleep from awareness, I continued to run, and to watch myself, perplexed. Who was this familiar stranger, efficiently motoring down the road on two legs? It was me, but it wasn't. At this time in my life, I couldn't have even walked briskly around the lake without a stretcher and IV fluids waiting for me at the finish.

Still, the image was so real and compelling, so satisfying, that I sat up and resolved to start running that day. Surely in a week or two, I could reenact my wonderful dream. How hard could it be? Every two-year-old knows how to run. And Lake Katherine wasn't that big; how far would it be to go around it? A mile? Two? Four?

I had no clear grasp of the length of a mile, but I decided to go for a run later in the day, as soon as I got home from work.

Work was *The Columbia Record,* which was an afternoon newspaper, if you can remember such things.

Yes, I am that old. I have been alive for so long that, in my first few years out of college, there was not only one newspaper in every city, but two. (Yes, I remember back-step milk deliveries, too.)

Being a journalist wasn't so much something I chose as something that happened to me. In the eighth grade, I won a schoolwide essay contest and came to the attention of David Knight, an enthusiastic young teacher who was the adviser of the school newspaper and was always looking for help.

Mr. Knight recruited me for the newspaper staff, introduced me to Strunk & White, and was a mentor to me throughout high school. I will always be grateful to him (and to the PE teacher who once picked me—*me!*—captain of a team) for believing in me.

And for never, ever once telling me I should lose ten pounds.

It's because of Mr. Knight's influence that, as a senior, I won a small scholarship and was named the SC Scholastic Press Association's Journalist of the Year.

Yes, I know. Alarmingly, this seems to indicate that, professionally, I peaked at seventeen and then should have retired and taken up knitting.

Instead I enrolled at the University of South Carolina to study journalism, demonstrating, like a bomb-sniffing hound, a shrewd ability to spot industries that will soon implode.

Even worse than choosing a dying profession for my major, I opted for the ten-year plan. I was already working as a reporter for a weekly newspaper and would soon be named editor of another. Since I was already employed in my field, college didn't seem like such a big deal, and I didn't apply myself. Computer science, for instance: Who's ever going to need that?

Regrets, I've had a few. Especially now, whenever I think wistfully of graduate school and take a look at my USC transcript.

Anyway, after five years of working for weeklies, the *Record* hired me as a copy editor. Thank you, Tom McLean and Bobby Hitt, for taking me on, despite my youth, my lack of experience, and the shockingly unnatural hue of my hair.

Being on the *Record* staff was a blast, the most fun on a job you can have at 6 AM. Since the paper was delivered in the afternoon, we were in early and finished by two. So by midafternoon on the day of my fateful dream, I was home and ready to begin training for my exhilarating run around Lake Katherine the next week.

Ah, ignorance. It does a body good.

I did, in fact, run that day. That is, if, by "running" you mean staggering down the road, with frequent stops, at the no-holds-barred pace of a snail.

At the time, I lived on a poorly paved road, about a mile long, about thirty minutes outside Columbia. On one end was a handful of modest single-family homes, which (unluckily for their inhabitants) looked out on my row of miserable duplexes.

The rest of the road was quiet and wooded, nothing but rough pavement flanked by scrub oaks. Except for the occasional passing car, there was no one to see me puff and jiggle. It was about a mile to the end of the street, and I figured there and back would make for an excellent run. My route, at least, was all set.

I fed the cats, including a litter of stray kittens living in the outside storage room, then looked for appropriate clothes.

I found a pair of gray sweatpants, an oversized T-shirt, and the only athletic shoes I owned at the time, white Tretorn tennis shoes with a jazzy blue stripe. I looked in the mirror. I looked more like a Walmart shopper than a runner, but it was good enough for government work. I headed out.

Tentatively, I loped to the end of my driveway—so far, so good—and began a slow, tortuous trot. Then a terrible thing happened.

As I jogged past the last house on the street, about fifty yards into my run, from inside an open window I heard someone whistle the first line of "Here Comes the Bride."

The tune was followed by laughter.

Now, I have absolutely no reason to believe those people were laughing at me. For all I knew, they were watching a rerun of *Sanford and Son* and Aunt Esther had just appeared on the screen.

But still. It *felt* like they were laughing at me, and the feeling was enough. My face grew hot. I was already out of breath, not even a quarter mile down the street. I probably looked like I'd just run fifty miles.

But in an unprecedented (for me) act of defiance and courage and lunacy, I kept going. For, really, what else *can* you do when you feel utterly humiliated, when it feels like the world is laughing at you? You can retreat, embarrassing yourself even further and giving aid and comfort to jerks, or stick your chin up, think *Screw you,* and keep going.

This is the truth: On this planet, small people are going to laugh at you, no matter what size you are or what you do. Small people thrive on derision, and unfortunately, they exist in large numbers.

Long before that first run, I was in a car with some other people, and we passed a fit but tired runner who looked like he was about to collapse. Somebody joked, "He doesn't look like he can make it to the end of the street." I remember thinking, *Yeah, but maybe he just finished twenty miles. When's the last time you ran twenty miles, bud?* But

I didn't know better then, so I said nothing. It bothers me to this day.

The rude comments made about me by passing motorists over the years are known only to them. For this, I am thankful for earbuds and exhaustion. When you're convinced that both of your legs are about to implode at the knee, you're focused on making it to the end of the street. You're not troubled by the amused glances and sardonic asides of the sedentary rubes.

And believe me, it's only the rubes who will laugh. Most runners will respect your effort, no matter how ungainly you seem.

I know this now, from experience. That first run, however, all I knew was I had no choice but to stick my chin up and keep going. Once I passed the homes, I could stop to walk and catch my breath every few minutes without anyone observing. In forty-five minutes, I jogged slowly to the end of the street and back, logging my first-ever two miles. It was the bravest thing I'll ever do.

No one whistled at me again, on that street or anywhere else. I've heard skinny female runners complain about drive-by lechery, which, to me, doesn't sound so bad. An occasional wolf whistle might be nice.

At various times in my life, I've ridden horses on public roads, and when I was much younger, leering men would occasionally slow and try to pick me up. (What they planned to do with the twelve-hundred-pound horse if I agreed to hop in was unclear; hope springs oblivious in the mind of a lecherous male.) But nobody ever hits on me while I'm out running and unencumbered by horse.

But I don't run to meet men. Nor—sigh—apparently to lose weight.

If I'd known then what I know now—that you can run a stinkin' half-marathon and weigh two pounds *more* when you get on the scale the next day—I may not have continued running. Back then, all I wanted to do was lose weight.

I ran because I thought if I were a runner, I would look like all the runners I knew: square-jawed, angular, *chiseled*. People like my Uncle Lloyd, who jumped out of airplanes in Vietnam and ran marathons for fun. A lean, mean fighting machine: That's the look I was after.

Oh, well.

It would be many years before the scale would come clean and whisper to me, "Run all you want, babe, but face it, you're *never* going to be thin." Didn't matter. By then, I was hooked. Hooked on those demon endorphins. I trained my evilest eye on the scale, kicked it, and said, "Like I care, buster."

I was lying, of course.

I do care. Always will, apparently. I climb on the scale every day.

four

What Not to Wear

On that very first run, I blew past my first obstacle to bliss, the phantom whistler.

But there loomed a larger, more sinister obstacle in my path—or rather, in my closet.

The full-length mirror.

Despite the difficulty of that first run, I was determined to repeat the experience. It wasn't because of how I felt when I ran; it was because of how I felt *afterward*. Accomplished. Virtuous. Clean.

It's like what Dorothy Parker said about her craft. She said she didn't like writing, but she liked having written. Likewise, when sedentary people first start to run, few enjoy the actual running. The reward comes later. The reward comes from *having* run.

That initial sense of accomplishment, coupled with the salty peace sweat leaves on your skin, made me decide to run every day. But decisions made in euphoria often look dumb when endorphins retreat. And my full-length mirror, conspiring with its evil twin (also known as my shadow), threatened daily to embarrass me back to a state of inertia. I would stand in front of it, looking with horror at what too many pizzas had wrought, and tread dangerously close to despair.

My closet held an adequate assortment of work clothes that serviceably covered up bulges. But you can't run in a plaid blazer and navy gabardine slacks. The quality of a run is dependent, in part, on the appropriateness of the clothes you wear.

I stood in front of the cruel mirror and tried on shorts, sweats, tights. Everything made me look fat. Of course it did. I *was* fat. And my long-dormant pride showed up, uninvited, and was screaming: *No way are you going outside looking like this for a walk, let alone a run! People will point! People will laugh! Woman, have you no shame?*

It was a dangerous time. In those first few weeks, despite my courageous first run, I knew too much derision could send me, whimpering, back to my pizzas and couch. I realized I couldn't look *good* struggling up the street at that weight, but I figured I could look less ridiculous.

A roomy fleece sweat suit with elastic at the ankles was good on occasion. (Understand: This was the 1980s.) But I lived in South Carolina, where people shop for Christmas trees with their convertible tops rolled down. Sweats wouldn't be an option for long, but neither were a skimpy pair of shorts and a sports bra.

When my hero, the writer George Sheehan, started running in the late 1960s, he wore only thin shorts, no shirt. Neighbors would ask Dr. Sheehan's mortified children why their father ran around town in his underwear.

Hah. Try running around town in your underwear, *fat*. Honestly, you skinny people have no idea.

Without the right clothes and generously applied lubricants, I wouldn't have kept running for two months. With jiggling arms, jellied thighs, and breasts flopping around like a couple of gasping fish on the floor of a boat, I wasn't a candidate for a Nike commercial.

I could have, however, inspired a reality show called Fanny 911.

Outfitting myself appropriately to run around public streets was a challenge. But there's no dilemma in life so difficult that a bumper sticker can't help us through. To wit: WHEN THE GOING GETS TOUGH, THE TOUGH GO SHOPPING.

I headed to the mall, where the first order of business was to acquire a sports bra. Actually, I bought two. It's called double-bagging, and it's a common procedure for women athletes of a certain chest size. Laugh all you want; two bras control more than one. Despite the recent development of some stunningly rigid chestware, to this day, if I'm running any distance of significance, I still double-bag. It's hell in the summer, but it keeps me out of courtrooms facing an obscenity charge.

To go atop the bras, I selected an extra-large, short-sleeved T-shirt. It was gray.

I know, I know.

Or, I should say: I know now.

Except for wool, cotton is the worst possible fabric to don if you're preparing to sweat. It sticks to every damp crevice, outlining your shape better than an airport-security scanner. Sure, it covers you, but it's not flattering. Had I run past Hooters in my damp T-shirt, its patrons wouldn't have looked up from their beers.

But it was ninety degrees in September, and a wet tee was better than a heavy sweatshirt. So for the first few months of running, this was my uniform: two sports bras, a Hanes Beefy-T, fleece sweatpants, Tretorn tennis shoes, and cotton footies with the little tassel ball on the back. (Note: Do not try this at home. Cotton footies grow corns, I think.)

Thus began a routine. Every day, when I got home from work, I took off my size 16–18 dresses and pulled on my running clothes. They disguised nothing. I would have looked the same size in an orange Spandex swimsuit two sizes two small.

But the T-shirt and sweats—when dry, anyway—felt light and airy, *athletic* even, and I needed that to get me out the door. It was the beginning of a lesson hard-earned: Sometimes, the feeling is better than the reality. And a kind fib can be morally superior to a haughty truth.

So, rayon Belle France dresses by day, cotton Hanes by night, my days looked something like this: work, run, sleep. I was not dating anyone at the time, had nothing dependent on me but four indifferent cats, and as LeAnn Rimes sings, I had nothing better to do.

And because the laws of science back then still held, I actually lost some weight—albeit slowly, like the pace of my runs. I couldn't run around Lake Katherine; was nowhere close to covering that distance. But after a year, I was down ten pounds; in another six months, down fifteen. Enough that people noticed, even though I'd told no one I was running.

"You look great," a co-worker said to me one day. "How much weight have you lost?"

Something thin people will never understand about fat people: Even the most well meaning of compliments can sting. They say, "Have you lost weight?" We hear, "Thank God, you've finally lightened up on the Krispy Kreme doughnuts."

We can't help it. When your body—which is your most private thing as well as your most public thing—has been the subject of a rude public commentary for decades, yeah, that spot is a little bit raw.

So I bristled.

I straightened myself up, sucked in my perpetually protruding gut, and said tartly, "That's kind of personal."

Sorry about that, Clif.

Look, all I'm saying is, use caution. The kindest thing to do, if a friend drops fifty pounds, is to say, "You look fantastic!" and leave it at that. Never, ever imply that your friend's weight was anything other than perfect for her height and genetically crafted big bones. Like reality, honesty is highly overrated.

There is nothing in the Ten Commandments about honesty, nothing except that you shouldn't bear false witness. And that doesn't mean you should be honest, only that you shouldn't lie. Those are two separate things.

I'm not advocating more dishonesty, just less honesty. I believe in the virtue of silence, of omission. Just because you think something doesn't mean you should say it.

But yes, it was true; I had lost some weight. As my hero George Sheehan once said, the running body tells you what it needs, and it turned out that mine did not need pizza. I started eating a bowl of cereal at night instead. I was nowhere near zipping that green silk dress, but I ventured back to the mall and found a turquoise workout suit, a polyester-cotton blend, with black-and-white zebra stripes down the sides. I thought I looked smokin' hot.

I bought two.

You could still hear me coming a quarter mile down the road, heralded by the noisy swish-swish of my thighs. But I was much cooler than I was in sticky fleece, and comfort paired with self-delusion made me feel like a freakin' gazelle.

So long as I didn't look down and spot my shadow.

five

A Reliable Source of Joy

In running, there are starting lines, and there are finish lines.

Then there's another line universal among runners, whether or not they ever enter a race—the Never-Going-Back-to-My-Old-Life line.

Once you cross it, you won't stop running until you are in jail, vegetative, or dead.

I crossed it about a year after I started running, the night something strange and wonderful occurred.

This didn't happen at the ugly old duplex. By then, I'd moved into a little house on two acres on another quiet, country road, also exactly two miles to the stop sign and back. (I wasn't aware of it yet, but I'd begun a lifetime practice of choosing homes based on the running conditions. Isolation is a plus, as is a wide road shoulder and a trailhead within a few miles.)

Anyway, Syrup Mill Road was the name. The running was so good here that, years later, when my new husband and I moved into a larger house in the city, I would sometimes drive an hour just to run thirty minutes on my old, friendly road. Syrup Mill Road and I, we were that thick.

It was here I was asked, for the first time (but, alas, not the last), if I needed assistance, if I needed a ride.

When it happens, I am, of course, wearing my old gray sweats.

It's an ordinary run to this point: From my house, to the end of the street, where I make the mistake of not stopping a moment to catch my breath. I'm still a novice runner, really, but trying to run consistently without stopping. I turn back for the final mile panting like an Alaskan husky in July. In the Deep South.

I'm also approaching a slight hill, so I slow to a shuffle, that not-quite-walking, not-quite-running gait you see when people are trying to get first in line at Walmart.

I hear the car before I see it. A Buick LeSabre, like my grandmother drives. It is missing a hubcap and, quite possibly, a muffler.

Shuffling along, looking straight ahead, I ignore its approach and maintain a steady tortoise pace on the side on the road.

The car slows.

Well, that's nice. When there's nothing but gravel between you and a four-thousand-pound sedan, it's always soothing to hear a driver slowing down.

The car passes me, slowly. That's good. But then, alarmingly, it stops.

Oh dear God. My mother was right. I *am* going to be murdered out here.

I think of turning around, running the other way, back toward the stop sign. But before I can pivot, a silvery head leans out the window.

What I've long suspected is true: Buick LeSabres are only driven by grandmothers.

Poor thing, she must be lost.

Relieved, I trot toward her, happy to be of assistance. But no. It's me she wants to assist.

"Honey, do you need a ride?" she says, squinting in concern. "Did you run out of gas? Do you want me to call someone?"

Startled and confused, I lunge to a stop.

"Um, no, thank you," I manage. "I'm . . . um . . . just running. Exercising."

From the expression on her face, I might as well have told her I was training for the Tour de France.

She waits, expectant of truth. Clearly, more is expected from me.

"It's just so hot today . . . And I'm kind of tired. So I guess I'm going slower than usual," I say lamely. "I'm fine. Really. I live just down the road a little." I gesture north.

Dubious, she watches the sweat drip from my forehead, catapult down two scarlet cheeks, and dive ecstatically into the folds of my damp, heaving chest.

"Oh, well," she says, after a minute. "You have a nice day, now, dear."

Well, that will not be possible now, will it? I think crossly to myself, freshly self-conscious as my would-be benefactor drives away.

Warning: We runners don't like to stop. It knocks us off schedule, messes up our rhythm, interrupts our runner's high.

And we really don't like to stop to be insulted.

But it's hard to stay indignant on the run. The endorphins beat the nasties out of you.

When I get home, I race to the front porch, flop on the stairs, and, after a moment, succumbing to the drive-by comedy of it all, howl with laughter. For all future offers of roadside assistance, I won't stop.

I'll just nod and wave.

But wait . . . that's not the strange and wonderful thing. This occurs a few months later.

By now, I am jogging two miles four or five times a week, usually at dusk. There are more mosquitoes at this hour but fewer onlookers, which seems like a pretty good trade-off to me.

Then one night, with no warning, it happens: a full moon. Ricky Skaggs in my earphones. And me, so alive, so exultant, after a perfect, strong, empowering run. So jacked up that when I reached my home, I dance, in the front yard. Me, leaping and twirling. Dancing for joy in the moon-silver grass.

Deep in the woods, happy frogs roar admiringly.

I'd danced before, but always awkwardly, self-consciously; always accompanied by that sly, ugly whispering in my head, the strains of childhood bullies hissing, *"You're fat."* This was the first time I'd ever danced freely, uninhibited, for nothing but the raw ecstasy of motion.

In the ABC television series *Lost,* the doomed character named Charlie makes a list of the top ten moments of his life. When I see that episode, I remember this night, that dance. I remember, and think, *That definitely would be on my list.*

For the first time in my life, I recognized that exertion, regardless of one's size, was a reliable source of joy.

Of course, exertion—well, running, at least—also happens to be hugely addictive. The longer and farther you run, the more it becomes a compulsion. This isn't just the babbling of a fat woman high on endorphins. There's actual science to back me up.

Virginia Grant and Bow Tong Lett, a pair of Canadian psychologists, have studied rats addicted to running and say their behavior is no different from rats addicted to morphine or cocaine.

Addicted rats will run twelve miles a day—nearly half a marathon, no small feat when your legs are half an inch long.

Give a rat a running wheel for twenty-three hours, and food for one hour, and he will literally starve himself to death, burning more calories than he can take in on his ratty little lunch break. It's runicide, a national rat tragedy. Somebody should notify PETA.

Even when not killing themselves, rats become cantankerous when deprived of their runs, the scientists observed. To anyone who has lived or worked with a runner, this explains a lot.

It explains people like Dean Karnazes, an ultramarathoner who has run 226 miles without stopping.

And Dave McGillivray, the Boston Marathon director who's too busy putting on the race to run in it, so he runs it himself, alone, later in the day.

It explains Richard Blaylock, a South Carolina engineer I read about, who had his lower right leg *amputated* because chronic pain from arthritis kept him from running. There was no medical reason for amputation. He's now running again, with metal and chrome from the shin down. He told a reporter, "I couldn't see a downside."

And it explains why, a few years ago, the Boston Marathon went on as scheduled even as a nor'easter bore down. The day before the race, *The Boston Globe* reported, "With a nasty brew of heavy rain, cold and headwinds forecast for Monday, authorities are scrambling to mitigate the misery of 23,000 runners in what could rank among the worst conditions of the Boston Marathon. More than 1,200 medical personnel will line the 26.2-mile course, waiting to treat runners for hypothermia or injuries."

Twenty thousand people finished that race, chafed, shivering, and beaming.

Which might lead the brat-eating spectator to pause, wipe the Sam Adams foam off his chin, and ask, in all seriousness: Are you people nuts?

No, we're not. We're addicts. We're addicted to serenity and joy.

Many trees have died so that *New York Times* health writer Gina Kolata and others can debate the existence of the runner's high and the role of endorphins in compelling athletes to compete and everyday folks like me to exercise regularly. But true things are usually simple and can be expressed in a dozen or so words. For me, this is the truth: When I exercise, I feel good. When I don't exercise, I don't.

Call me kooky, zany, nutty, but I prefer to feel good, always have. So as the years went on, I kept running.

I ran up and down Syrup Mill Road, around high school tracks, over dusty dirt roads meandering through state parks.

I ran as I reconnected with a boy I'd known in high school, got engaged and got married, changed jobs, turned thirty. I ran as I had a child and then three, then four.

I ran in North Carolina, Maryland, Virginia. Charleston, Potomac, Richmond. I ran as our hardy little family moved eleven times in twelve years, each time moving farther away from my old sedentary life, my family of origin, and my darling first home on Syrup Mill Road. I ran from old, painful memories. I ran to explore strange new cities.

The only time I wasn't running was when I was pregnant, and it was only because I was throwing up so much.

The experts say each pregnancy is different, but mine all followed a pattern: Euphoria. A vow to keep running the whole nine months. Then debilitating nausea that kept me unwillingly sedentary until the baby emerged.

I tried ginger ale, ginger capsules, gingersnaps. I wore air-sickness bands. I consumed twice my weight in saltines. The doctor prescribed pills and suppositories. Nothing worked. I would stagger through the bare minimum of the day's responsibilities, then when my husband got home, I'd thrust the kids/cats/dishes at him and curl up, moaning, in bed.

In each pregnancy, there would be a few things I could eat at a certain time of day. With Galen, it was a McDonald's sausage-and-egg platter between 9 and 10 AM. With Katherine, Chinese chicken with mushrooms in the early afternoon. The womb gave orders and I obeyed, lest I find myself retching on some innocent shrub.

I would like to take this opportunity to make a long-overdue apology to the fine people who do the landscaping at the Sullivan's Island town park.

You'd think, wouldn't you, that I might have lost weight back then, or at least not gained sixty pounds in each pregnancy. Oh, no. I am a champion at gaining weight, even when I'm throwing up. I gained sixty pounds in my first pregnancy, and had lost only twenty of them when I turned up pregnant again eleven months later.

Naively, I thought that being pregnant would make me immune to fat jokes. It is, after all, the one time in a woman's life when she's *encouraged* to gain weight.

But no.

Once, eight months' pregnant, I was walking into the newspaper office, wearing a blue denim jumper loaned to me by a friend, and thinking I looked rather cute.

When I approached the front desk, there was a school group there—middle schoolers waiting to take a tour of the printing plant. I smiled at the teacher, waved at the security guard, and walked on. And then I heard one of the boys in line say—loudly, unmistakably, triumphantly—"Free Willy!"

It was "Here Comes the Bride," redux.

I kept walking, but felt my face redden. I waited for the elevator, praying no one would be in it, feeling tears leak in my eyes. I wanted to turn around, stomp back to that rotten kid, and yell, *Can't you see I'm pregnant? I'm* supposed *to look like this.*

But I didn't. Not only because I was a nice southern girl, but because that wasn't true.

Not everyone who is eight months' pregnant looks like a killer whale. Demi Moore, nude on the cover of *Vanity Fair* in 1991, sure didn't.

I loved getting pregnant and having babies, but gestation reminded me of those dreadful early years when I wasn't a fat runner, just fat. Mercifully, each pregnancy ended at the appointed time, and before the baby slept through the night, I'd be back on the street, pushing a purple Baby Jogger my friend Carol gave me, and, for a time, wearing an aging and tattered pair of gray fleece sweatpants.

Addiction can be a good thing, sometimes. Rats like us, baby, we were born to run.

six

On Your Mark

My hero George Sheehan said the difference between a runner and a jogger is an entry blank, but I'd been running for ten years before I summoned up enough nerve to enter a race.

It was a Thanksgiving Day Turkey Trot. Seemed apropos at the time.

Later experience with wild turkeys taught me they really have just two speeds: amble, and get-me-outta-here, at which time they fly up a tree. Despite their gawky appearance, turkeys have a degree of dignity that evades horses and the human running population. They don't trot. But that's exactly what most people in a road race do.

The business of road racing is a triumph of capitalism, equivalent in genius only to Sam's Club or BJ's Wholesale. Who'd have thought the American people, many of them graduates of fine universities, would *pay* to get to *buy* something in a store?

Who'd have thought they'd pay to run down a public street?

But that's what we do, in large numbers. Local 5Ks typically charge fifteen or twenty dollars to participate. The big marathons, like Boston and New York, are approaching two hundred dollars for an entry. I would say "only in America," but no—the Berlin and London marathons are pricier, and they, too, always sell out.

I have a friend who's about to run the Boston Marathon for the ninth time. If running in itself is addictive, road racing is even more so. The fastest way to get hooked on running? Enter a neighborhood 5K, even if you just walk.

As for me, I'd like to say I prepared for my first race by training hard, eating healthily, and gradually increasing my mileage, like the running magazines recommend.

But of course not.

It was the fourth Tuesday in November, and I was on the phone, coordinating with relatives the time for our Thanksgiving feast.

"Lloyd and Stephanie are running in the Turkey Trot," my aunt told me, "so we can't get together before noon."

Lloyd, you may recall, is my marathoning/paratrooper/man-of-steel uncle. Stephanie is his daughter, my first cousin, who was born in Buenos Aires and has always been—and will always be—much younger, thinner, and prettier than me.

But my uncle's pace was slowing, and Stephanie, as far as I knew, ran only on occasion. Meanwhile, I was up to three miles, three or four times a week.

We were living in Charleston, South Carolina, then, and my third child was a year old. Every morning, after my husband left for work and the older kids walked to school, I'd do the household chores, then bundle Galen into his car seat and load the Baby Jogger in my black Jeep Cherokee. Then we'd be off to explore some running paradise.

We'd run laps around the lake at James Island County Park. Past the silent cannons at Charleston Harbor's Battery. Or, when the tide was low and the sand firm, we'd cover three or four miles at Folly Beach, both of us turning blonder and browner in the late-morning sun. Sometimes Galen would fall asleep in the stroller, and I'd run longer so I wouldn't have to wake him. I'd squat and kiss his cheek, salty from the sea air, and take off again, even more slowly and gently this time.

Another of the top ten moments of my life? One of those runs, definitely.

But we interrupt this blissful reverie to return to Thanksgiving.

As my aunt and I talked, I realized that, for the first time, I was as much of a "real" runner as my uncle and beautiful cousin, even though I probably outweighed them by a good seventy-five pounds.

And yet *they* were going to run the Turkey Trot, while I peeled potatoes at home?

Envy banged on my door, and its voice was shrill and petulant.

"Turkey Trot? *Turkey Trot? I* want to be in a Turkey Trot," my inner snot whined as I hung up the phone.

"Well, okay, then, go register and run in it," my higher self answered reasonably, getting back to the dinner at hand.

The Knights of Columbus Turkey Trot is a 5K—that's 3.1 miles, only a little longer than my usual routes. The distance was not daunting. The company was. Running in a crowd of people—worse, running in a crowd of *runners,* who were, in my mind, not so much *people* as thick-calved Greek gods—intimidated the hell out of me.

What if I finished last? What if I couldn't finish at all? What would I wear? How would I look? What if someone asked if I needed a ride?

I didn't know then that the typical road race is more inclusive than a Unitarian church. The organizers don't care who registers or who runs, so long as you show up with the cash. I also didn't know then that, in every race I ran, I'd pass skinny people. And that I'd never finish last.

All I knew was that Stephanie was running, and by God, if she was going to sit at the Thanksgiving table wearing a TURKEY TROT T-shirt, well then, so was I.

The next morning, I hied myself over to the Knights of Columbus Hall, paid my money, signed my waiver, got my T-shirt. My racing career had begun.

Oh, all right. Not *racing.* My career of jogging in a group while watching for potholes had begun.

Let's be honest. A road race is an actual race only for the fifty or so people at the front. The rest of us are just hoping to finish, hoping to beat our last time, hoping to beat the fat woman in Spandex in front of us, or, in my case, hoping that we're running in the right race.

True story: Five years after my first Turkey Trot, I accidentally ran in the wrong race.

How does this happen? (Why does a man steal a vacuum cleaner?) It's mostly because I was late.

We'd recently moved to Richmond, Virginia, a nice enough small southern city if you like small southern cities, as I do. With no family nearby, we had no plans for Thanksgiving Day that didn't involve gravy, and so—an old hand at this now—I'd registered for the local Turkey Trot. It was to be held near the University of Richmond, in an area of the city I'd never been. And I was thrilled to learn a portion of the course was on a wooded trail. In previous races, I'd only run on roads.

Because no one else wanted to spend Thanksgiving morning waiting for sweaty, skinny people (and me) to run through the woods, the rest of the family opted to stay home and watch the Macy's parade. We'd eat when I got back.

I was making my grandmother's legendary corn bread dressing for the first time, and so I left the house a little late. Nonetheless, MapQuest assured me I'd be there in plenty of time.

MapQuest lies.

The race was on Wheeler Street, and I turned onto it minutes before the start. Thanks be to God, there it was. A row of Porta-Potties, and a throng of people milling about in shorts. Whew. I parked in the first space I could find and sprinted to the back of the crowd, getting there literally at the moment someone yelled "Go!"

Tragically, there was no time for a Porta-Potty stop.

But you pay your money, you run your race. Bladder howling, I threw myself into it.

Then about half a mile in—for those of you keeping score at home, at my pace, that would be about six minutes later—I looked at another runner's bib and noticed it looked different from mine. Different color. Different type.

Oh, well, maybe the early entrants got different bibs than those who registered later.

But no. Another runner came near, and I looked closer. Different *words.*

Mayday, mayday.

And—wait a minute—we were running on a paved bike path. Where were these vaunted wooded trails?

Okay, keep calm, I thought frantically. *It is Thanksgiving, isn't it?* Check. There was a turkey in the oven back at home.

Panting, I looked around for someone who looked nice. A mile into a 10K, it's not always easy to find someone eager to chat.

Only, it turns out, it *wasn't* a 10K. That race, the one I'd registered for, was half a mile farther down the road.

It turned out, there are *two* freakin' Turkey Trots in Richmond, Virginia, on Thanksgiving (who knew?) and—could somebody please explain this to me?—both start *on the same road.*

At least I'd registered for the 10K and stumbled into a 5K. It really would have been a crisis if it'd been the other way around.

As it was, my only problem now, other than my aching bladder, was running in shame, being a bandit for the first time in my life.

Bandits are people who run in races for which they are not registered. They do it either because they're cheap and don't want to pay to run down a city street that they, as a taxpayer, ostensibly own (an entirely reasonable position to take). Or because they couldn't qualify for the race, or they waited too long to register and the race closed and they couldn't score a bib number on Craigslist.

Regardless of reason, these are bib-less people who take cover in the crowd before the gun goes off.

Some races are tolerant of bandits. The Cooper River Bridge Run in Charleston, for example, has a special chute at the end that says BANDITS EXIT HERE so they won't clog the finish line earned by the legitimate racers.

I think. Either that, or there are police officers waiting at the bandit chute, waiting to whisk them away.

I wouldn't know. I cower in the face of authority, so I would never deliberately run as a bandit.

Undeliberately, however . . .

Of course, I was wearing a race number, and the casual observer probably wouldn't have noticed the discrepancy. The way I *felt,* however, I might as well have been wearing a jester's hat in the Festival of Fools.

Not that it ultimately mattered.

When I neared the finish, I ducked off to the side and sheepishly told the chip-takers I was in the wrong race. The race officials never looked twice. There are times when it pays to be a fat runner.

Amazingly enough, that wasn't my strangest race ever. That dubious honor goes to a race in which I didn't actually run: the Jack London 10K Trail Race in Nashua, New Hampshire.

I registered for this race ignoring some enormous red flags. Flag one: It was early in the morning. Flag two: In another state. Flag three: On November 1.

That would be November 1, as in the day after Halloween.

Have I mentioned I have four kids?

As anyone with either (a) *kids* or (b) *a brain* might have predicted, I did not show up for the Jack London Trail Race.

But amazingly enough, I set a personal record!

A few months later, a friend who lives in New Hampshire emailed me the results of the race with a note saying, "Wow! That was fast!"

According to the official race website, I had indeed run that race. There I was: Jennifer Graham, forty-seven, of Hopkinton, Massachusetts. And I'd finished in a blistering forty-nine minutes, twenty-six seconds. That's an average pace of just under eight minutes per mile.

Now for those of you keeping score at home, my usual pace is between twelve and thirteen minutes per mile, depending on the number of hills, the amount of ice on the road, and if there are any wildflowers that I need to stop and collect. My Fastest Mile Ever, according to Lance Armstrong, who keeps up with these things on my magic iPod, was ten minutes, seven seconds. But I'm pretty sure my magic iPod was malfunctioning that day.

Day in, day out, I'm a solid twelve-minute miler, and that's on a straight, flat road, not on a challenging trail.

A nine-minute pace in a 10K trail run would have been an extraordinary achievement for a fat runner like me. I'd have notified all kith and kin that very day.

An eight-minute pace would have required condolences to the immediate family, as I would have collapsed before the quarter-mile mark.

It was obvious, though, what had happened. When I didn't show up, some unregistered runner helped herself (or himself) to my number. Which, quite honestly, is just fine. If anyone would like to run in my place to, say, qualify for Boston, you go right ahead. Just save me the T-shirt.

So see, there's big adventure waiting for you out there in the world of road racing. There's always a Shirtless Wonder who will glare if you get in his way, but for the most part it's a friendly, accommodating place. Lots of sweat, yes, but no statistically significant blood or tears. I urge you to join us, if you're not already out there.

And my first race, that Turkey Trot I was so nervous about entering? I didn't beat Uncle Lloyd and Stephanie, but I finished without walking a step. It was a small event by road-racing standards: no timing chips, no bands, no spectators, and, mercifully, no finish-line photography. The only picture of me in my zebra-striped jacket and black tights is filed away in my mind.

If you could see it, you'd see I'm smokin' hot.

seven

Kiawah

Thirty miles from the proud steeples that give the Holy City of Charleston its nickname are two islands. Wildish, private, and closed to pesky interlopers, they're much like my introverted hero George Sheehan.

Kiawah and Seabrook islands have gates. You can't get past the security guards unless you own property, are renting a condo, or are participating in an event for which you have a pass.

Most of my childhood vacations took place on the free public beaches in Charleston. But when I was a teen, my mother remarried, and sometimes she and my stepfather would take me to Seabrook Island for the weekend. The price of admission—a condo rental—was steep, but worth it for one thing: the shells.

Usually the public beaches of South Carolina are picked clean of good shells by noon every day, unless a storm has upended the ocean floor. But at the private islands, where access is restricted, shells are plentiful. Bull's-eyes, conchs, whelks, augers, cockles, and lettered olives. All whole and pristine.

Sometimes I wonder if resorts hire people to dump manufactured shells on the beach while people are sleeping, like the Easter Bunny scattering eggs.

At Seabrook, we found sand dollars. Buckets of them. Call them sea biscuits or sand dollars, to me they're the only creatures more beautiful when they're dead.

Alive, they're greenish brown and icky, with waving, fine hairs called cilia that grotesquely cover their spines. In South Carolina, it's illegal to take a living sea creature, even if it washed up on the shore, so when we find them in sand we scoop them up carefully, recoiling from the feel of them, and gently release them in deep water.

We tell them to come back when they're dead.

Dead, they're exquisite.

The rational mind resists the irrational notion that this dainty, pale disk is a skeleton. Relieved of its dark, furry cilia, an unbroken sand dollar looks like some, exotic holy thing manufactured in another galaxy. It is a sun-bleached sphere—a tiny flat moon—with a ring of oval pores that dance in perfect symmetry around a five-petaled flower.

Some people call them mermaid money. I am no more mermaid than marathoner, but I deal in their currency. These days, I offer my kids five dollars for every sand dollar they find.

Other people have skeletons in their closets. Mine are all over the house.

If Seabrook means sand dollars to me, Kiawah means driftwood.

On my first visit there, I walk the beach at dusk and scoop up mounds of it. It seems important, somehow. Maybe this piece was part of a schooner that sank a century ago. Maybe this was the leg of a pre–Civil War chair. It looks like the splinters of giants. It smells dead.

I try to think of uses for it, but I can think of no place in my home where it wouldn't look like an ordinary piece of wood, broken and discolored. Context is everything. I leave it on the beach. Where it's supposed to be. Where it's lovely, among friends.

I've been to Kiawah Island exactly four times in my life. Neither I nor my parents—nor my ancestors, for that matter—have Kiawah money. We're devotees of funky, down-home Folly Beach, South Carolina's Mayberry-by-the-Sea.

But once, Michael and I and the kids shared a condominium there with his sister and her family for the weekend. Then I got the idea I needed to run a half-marathon, and Kiawah seemed like the perfect place to start.

I can say with confidence Kiawah is the best half-marathon on the planet because of three things:

One, the course is flat.

Two, they serve hot bean soup at the post-race buffet.

Three, both marathoners and half-marathoners get the same shirt. This means I own a Kiawah Island *Marathon* shirt even though I can only run 13.1 miles.

Is this a great country, or what?

I've run Kiawah a couple of times now, but, like sex, the first time is what you remember. Up until then, I'd participated in a grand total of three races, the longest of which was six miles. There was my first Turkey Trot. Then another 5K, the Charleston Reindeer Run. And then the 10K Cooper River Bridge Run, which, since we're being honest, I must confess, I walked with my best friend.

Before Kiawah, I'd never run thirteen miles at one time.

So, to prepare, I planned to do what the experts recommend: Train hard and build slowly, increasing the distance of my weekly long run by no more than 10 percent each week.

(Insert uproarious laughter.)

The experts don't have babies.

When you have young children, you run when you can. So, running as much as I could—say, when no one had the croup or had to construct a diorama—I built up to six miles, maybe six and a half, the week before the race. That was going to have to do. I had no idea if I'd be able to finish on race day, no idea what would happen if I had to drop out.

Would they send an ambulance for me? A limo? Who knows how they pick up spent runners on Kiawah's palmetto-lined streets? Would they even let emergency medical technicians on the island for the purpose of retrieving a fallen fat runner?

For that matter, would they even let a fat runner loose on the course?

Rich people are notoriously skinny. You can't be too rich, too thin, or too condescending; that's what I hear. Being fat, therefore, is a proclamation of my lower-middle-class proclivities. Maybe they'd take one look at me, give me an apron, and direct me to the buffet line to ladle out the hot bean soup.

I had concerns.

I also had no condominium in which to stay.

I had a day pass for the island, which meant even if the stern security guard waved me in, I'd have to leave the Jeep in the parking lot farthest from the starting line. Then wait and wait and wait to catch a shuttle to get to the main tent.

But you pay your money, you run your race.

On your mark, get set.

Race day dawns. I leave the house while everyone is sleeping and drive twenty miles from my James Island house to the Kiawah gate. I park and nervously collect my belongings: water bottle, car key, emergency cash, timing chip, and bib. I lock the car and head to the back of the shuttle line.

Egad. The place is infested with skinny people. Skinny people in short shorts.

I look down at my black Lycra capris, the inner thighs worn and slightly pilled. I feel thick. Congealed. Like a fruit salad my grandmother makes with Jell-O and cottage cheese.

As I wait, I listen to the conversations around me. A diminutive woman in front of me is talking with her two diminutive adult daughters, planning what race they will run next. Behind me, a man and a woman are stretching their hamstrings and gazing at each other like lovesick puppies.

They couldn't care less about my thighs.

In fact, it becomes increasingly clear, nobody cares about my thighs but me. Everyone is thinking about their own thighs, or the thighs of their girlfriends stretching their lovely long hamstrings, or, more likely, the terrifyingly long distance we are all about to race.

Thinking about these things, me and the skinny people catch our shuttle. We disembark at the tent. We wait in line for an open Porta-Potty, jog anxiously in place to keep warm. We double-check the safety pins on our bibs. And then, when the national anthem is sung and the gun goes off, me and the skinny people start running.

We run slowly. We have to, to keep from running into one another.

For the first mile or two, we all shuffle along in a densely packed herd. We look vaguely like the throng pushing through the doors of

Walmart at 4 AM on Black Friday. Only nicer. We trample no one.

At Miles 3 and 4, space opens up. Some people stop for water; others visit a Porta-Potty that pops up occasionally on the course.

The breathing gets louder.

For very fit people, the first few miles is just a warm-up.

For not-very-fit people, people for whom three miles is usually their whole workout—people like, say, me—this is the point at which they start to breathe so others can hear them.

My breathing embarrasses me. I try to keep it quiet, so as not to notify others that I am in no way prepared to run 13.1 miles. To distract myself from my breathing. Eventually, though, it becomes rhythmic, like the rub of my thighs, and it is lost in the pain and the struggle and, at times, terrible boredom. The race seems to go on forever.

But then me and the skinny people and a few other ecstatic fat people I encountered out there . . . all of us (well, most all of us) finished the race.

Finished, did you hear?

Me, in my scruffy tights and my Hanes Beefy-T, ran 13.1 miles, without stopping. True, I was in agony for the last three miles, and I had blisters for the next two weeks, and I'm pretty sure someone played a cruel trick on us and changed the signage so that the last hundred yards was actually five miles.

But I finished, enjoyed a bagel and a bowl of hot bean soup, which I'm pretty sure was made in God's kitchen. Then I hobbled back to the bus and eventually got back to my car.

On the way home to James Island, I pulled through the McDonald's drive-through and got French fries, a large. Needed to replenish my sodium.

For some reason, the next morning when I got on the scale, I'd gained two pounds.

How is that even possible? It was a large fries, sure, but I'd just run for nearly three stinkin' hours.

It's okay. I don't run to lose weight.

Apparently, just to lose men.

eight

Neither Rain, Nor Snow, Nor Catheters

In case you're wondering why we moved so much, why I run up and down the East Coast like an I-95 trucker, it's because my husband was in talk radio.

Or, I suppose I should say, my *former* husband *is* in talk radio. Divorce wreaks havoc with your tenses. Among other things.

Before we were married, Michael had been a stand-up comedian, but he'd grown tired of living on the road. After his first marriage ended, he returned to Columbia, where his family lived, and where we'd met ten years earlier, when we were both in high school.

It all seemed providential, like a fortuitous closure of a circle. Our first date was at an International House of Pancakes in sight of the coffeehouse where we'd first met.

Later, when things turned serious, and it was time for our parents to meet, IHOP loomed large again, which is vaguely troubling in the grand scheme of things. Shouldn't the landmarks of a life well lived be, say, the Guggenheim or the Champ de Mars?

IHOP? This is the best I can do?

Apparently so.

For Christmas, we both gave our parents tickets to see the comedian/columnist Lewis Grizzard perform at the Koger Center in Columbia. Then we asked them to meet us at IHOP for coffee after the show. We didn't tell them the other parents were going, too.

Or that they'd be sitting next to each other.

On that fateful evening, Michael and I arrived at IHOP early, ordered coffee and tea, and spent the next fifteen minutes envisioning the fistfight our mothers were having. It had seemed like such a good idea at the time. But suddenly we realized the many ways in which things could go wrong.

What if, for example, my stepfather announced to the affable man in the next seat that he didn't like the bum his daughter was dating? What if Michael's mother had chimed in, "Oh, I know what you mean . . . my son is seeing this idiot reporter with Dolly Parton hair"?

What if, during the long intermission, they'd eventually figured things out?

In the back booth at the Assembly Street IHOP, tension was rising like a balloon drifting toward a thumbtack. We fidgeted. We drummed the table. We called for refills. Outside the window, traffic picked up. Clearly, the show was over.

Five minutes passed. Ten minutes. No parents.

Not mine. Not his.

A police car drove by. Then an ambulance.

Oh dear God, we've murdered our parents. As Lewis Grizzard would have said, they tore out each other's hearts and stomped those suckers flat. We will be tried and convicted of parricide by proxy and spend the rest of our lives in jail, where there is no boysenberry syrup.

But then, our parents walked in. All four, alive and oblivious. At the show, they'd talked to each other, as we'd thought, but the conversation was pleasant and benign. We had to explain to them separately why the nice couple from the Koger Center had inexplicably turned up here. We had a good laugh. The delicate business of merging families was off to a good start.

Two years later, we all gathered at Rutledge Chapel on the University of South Carolina campus, where Michael and I promised "for better or worse."

The reception was at the USC Faculty House, but I see now we should have had it at IHOP. Things go badly when you try to tamper with fate.

After the wedding, Michael moved into my little house on Syrup Mill Road, and I continued to work at the newspaper, while he tried his hand at politics for a few years. Occasionally, he'd be a guest on WBT, a powerhouse talk station in Charlotte, and the program director was impressed. When a part-time evening slot came open, Michael was invited to audition for it.

My mother and I could just barely pick up the signal in her home eighty miles away from Charlotte, but if we jiggled the antenna and held the radio near the kitchen window, we could hear. He sounded good. Sharp, funny, comfortable. He got the job the next week.

Despite the hour-long commute, for Michael the transition seemed easy enough. Both comedians and talk-show hosts, after all, are entertainers. Same genus, different species. Kind of like dogs and wolves.

For me, though, it took a while to adjust, to both the schedule and the notoriety. I quickly discovered a hidden suffering class in America: the wives of radio talk-show hosts.

Seriously, these women need organized protection. They're more threatened than the piping plover. They're not just wives and mothers; they are their husbands' show prep. Their flaws, their foibles, their cooking, their sex lives—everything's fodder for the air. Just ask Tania Beck, whose efforts to conceive a child were detailed hilariously on husband Glenn's national radio show.

On Michael's show, I became known as The Warden. Although I was rarely on the show—having learned early on not to answer the phone when he was on the air—I was a regular character there.

Everywhere we went, people would shake his hand, then look at me and say, "So, is this The Warden?" Feebly, I'd try to point out that if I were really warden-like, he'd be too scared to call me that on the air, but no one seemed to get it.

After a while, I suggested that Michael call me his "lovely bride," which is what our broadcaster friend John Wrisley called *his* wife on the air. And Michael finally consented.

From then on, he called me "my lovely bride, The Warden."

Like I said, a suffering class.

Talk radio is a volatile industry, and if you're any good at it, you can find yourself fired up the ladder to success.

Sure enough, every time Michael was fired, he wound up with a better job.

First, he was fired in Charlotte, for joking that the Columbine shooters were, at least, picking off athletes.

This was while the Columbine shootings were still going on.

(In his defense, he was live, he was a rookie, and he didn't know how bad the carnage would be.)

Still, in any other profession, make a joke like that, and you'd be slinging burgers the rest of your life. But this is talk radio, remember? There's nothing you can say so egregious you can't find another good job.

Of course, there were no offers from Colorado, but other radio stations called with openings they had. Of the lot, he picked Charleston, South Carolina, and within two weeks we were moving again.

Unfortunately, we'd bought a house three months earlier. But this was back when houses were still worth something, and so we were able to sell quickly without losing any money. I packed, pregnant. We lived in Charleston for three glorious years.

Then came an offer from a new station in Washington DC.

In June. We had to leave Charleston in June. No more sunny beach runs for Galen and me.

To cushion the blow, Michael found us a darling home with gingerbread trim in the woods of Potomac, Maryland.

I packed, pregnant.

I was turning forty, seven months' pregnant with my fourth child, and moving again.

Don't ever tell me I wasn't crazily in love with this guy.

Katherine was born in September, and Michael was let go three months later. Creative differences, I think it was.

This time, we landed in Richmond.

I complained, of course, but good-naturedly. Truth is, once I got over Syrup Mill Road, I took to moving joyously. Constant moving has many things to recommend it. For one thing, the house never gets really dirty. You get changes of color and view and wallpaper, and it is an absolute imperative—not a crazy female whim—that the furniture be rearranged.

And of course, moving means new places to run. New races, new routes, new climates. Having lived in the South for thirty years, I wasn't sure how I would adapt. In South Carolina, there are two temperatures: warm and hot. They say the only thing between Columbia and hell in August is a screen door.

But hallelujah, it turns out I *like* to run in the cold. I like all weather extremes. This is because there's nobody else out there, and so I get to feel reckless and noble.

There aren't many opportunities for people who live in the suburbs to feel noble these days, unless you can expertly compost.

But I, fat runner and boring suburban stay-at-home mother of four, have run outside when the temperature was one hundred degrees Fahrenheit. I have run outside when it was six degrees and the wind was blowing in gusts of thirty-five miles an hour. Regrettably, I have never had the pleasure of running at temperatures below zero, but not for lack for desire. It just doesn't get that cold where I live.

But I do run in snow, and when the roads are blotchy with ice. And if you don't, let me warn you: The few, the frozen, the addicted like me are out there. For your own sake, and that of your insurance company, please get out of our way.

My adventures as an extreme runner began in Richmond, where there is snow, but not in disagreeable amounts. Maybe once or twice a year, we'd get six inches, leaving us a wintry tableau that would be pretty if it didn't look so much like an ER visit waiting to happen.

Richmond, being the capital of the Confederacy and all, isn't as effective at snow removal as the picturesque towns of New England. Of course, I'm not so great at negotiating snow, either. Growing up in the South will do that to you. I still can't squelch the ripple of alarm I feel when I see a car going down the road when snow is falling. Don't they know how dangerous snow is?

In Columbia, it's martial law at first flake.

But in Richmond, as in Boston, life goes on when it snows. Businesses stay open; school is in session. The roads are salted and sanded.

But not the bike paths on which I run.

The snow on them melts during the day, and then freezes at night. They're impassable on foot for much of the winter. The track at the middle school is the same. All my running routes turn to frozen tundra.

So what's a runner to do?

Some might say, don't run. Take a break. Kick back. Embrace your inner sloth.

Those people don't live in my house.

The people who live in my house know that my daily three-miler keeps the beast at bay, and my cheerfulness, industry, and willingness to pick up dirty socks off the floor without exploding is in direct proportion to the number of miles run that week. So as soon as the precipitating stops, they're pushing me out the door.

Problem is, there's nowhere to run but the road.

And so begins the winter ritual of Runner's Roulette, in which exercise addicts like myself face down three-ton Range Rovers on slick surfaces. Why Fox hasn't picked this up yet is a mystery to me. It's a much better premise than irritable chefs.

I begin cautiously, trotting down the road as close to the icy edge as I dare. Every time a minivan emerges on the horizon, I hop to the side of the road and wait on the ice, meekly offering the right-of-way as if the passing cars were steel-and-fiberglass gods due homage. I do this for half a mile or so, but then, empowered by the cold and exertion, I get cocky.

I remember the February issue of *Runner's World* and its "Tips for Cold-Weather Running."

"Make running dates with your buds! This force feeds you out into the cold, where the weather-cursing and collective 'Yeah, we BAAAAAD!' boasting will take your mind off the temps," the author said.

I have no running buds, but the attitude, I happily adopt.

"Yeah, I BAAAAAD!" I chant, throwing my shoulders back and taking up a bit more of the road. The next time a gray Taurus heads toward me, I look defiantly at the driver and don't budge an inch off the pavement.

Inside the warm car, the driver puffs a cigarette and looks contemptuously at me. I know what he's thinking: *Yeah, you IDIOTTTT!*

I am undeterred. I have the moral high ground, if not the right-of-way. I am, after all, *exercising*, and it's fourteen stinkin' degrees outside. Heck, anybody can get in a car and go to work. I am Rocky Balboa— III or is it IV?—in Russia, training his tough self in the snow.

Eventually, I brazenly run in the center of the lane, trusting my senses to alert me to all coming interlopers. I duck to the side only on the rare occasion when there's a car in each lane, and I can't take the chance of those sedentary morons, distracted by my machismo, plowing into each other. Mentally, however, I start taking inventory.

Green Jeep, luggage rack on top, I think, as an SUV heads toward me. White Mercedes, early '80s coupe, OBX sticker on back.

I want to be able to identify the person who hit me when they load me onto the stretcher.

I doubt it will be an accident. I smell animosity in the chill air, but I'm unable to quell it. The endorphins, they've taken over.

Twenty minutes later, having turned around and safely heading for home, I finally encounter another runner. It's a woman, about my age, though barely identifiable under multiple layers of Gore-Tex. She, too, is running on the road, and in the universal greeting of runners, we nod at each other without breaking a stride.

Our shared noble effort, however, seems to call for more.

"It's not so bad out here," I say bravely, even as a school bus bears down upon us. She says something, but I don't hear; the words are lost under her scarf.

I think she said, "We're baaadddd." Honestly, who needs a bike path, anyway?

There are some people who think that runners are snobs. These people are called non-runners. And they're right, of course. There is a certain hubris you develop when you do things no one else does.

Like running in ice.

Or running with a catheter strapped to your leg.

She doesn't know this, and please don't tell her, but Katherine, my fourth child, nearly did me in.

When she was born via C-section (my fourth), something went wrong. A lot of my blood spilled on the floor. I remember very little of what transpired over the next few days.

What I remember: Lying on a gurney in a recovery room, and feeling blood gush between my legs. The doctor telling my husband he would have to operate again.

I remember counting backward from ten and waking up in the intensive care unit, with my hands strapped to the bed. A TV blaring, and old nurses bathing me, and tubes everywhere, in my mouth, in my arms. I remember people coming into my draped cubicle to show Katherine to me, her sweet pink rosebud baby face hoisted up in front of me, because I wasn't allowed, or able, to hold her.

I remember tears in my eyes as they carried her away.

I had a condition called placenta previa, in which the placenta grows over the cervix. I'd had this in my third pregnancy, too, but without complication. This time, my luck ran out. The tissue tore, and I hemorrhaged. Then part of my bladder ripped open, and another surgeon was called in. When I went home ten days later, I had a catheter that I had to wear for a month.

All you healthy people, you have no idea what it's like to run with a catheter taped to your leg. Weighing 216 pounds.

My recovery was slow. I'd needed twenty-three pints of blood in the hospital. For six months, I had searing pain in my throat when I exercised, thanks to the tube in my throat. For a year, I had recurrent infections and inflammation in places I'd rather not discuss. I'd been so sick for a while that friends from South Carolina and Georgia arrived. One brought a black dress. So sick that a priest was on call, just in case.

Even now, there are days I'm not so sure I *didn't* die, that everything that has happened since then has been part of some hellish purgatory, and that all of you are just bit players in my punishment, and we're all going to congregate anytime now in a church with Christian Shephard and the entire cast of the TV show *Lost*.

But the catheter eventually came out, and Katherine eventually slept through the night, and I ran and starved myself back to a waiflike 180 pounds. Two months after her first birthday, I was well enough to run in the wrong race. A year later, vigorous enough to run a half-marathon, and uninhibited enough to let a strange man run his hands all over my body.

nine

Our Bodies, Ourselves, Our Masseurs

The experts say runners should get regular massages, that vigorous kneading of muscle and tissue protects against future injury and cuts recovery times in half.

I agree wholeheartedly. Foggy and Jo-Jo do not.

Where I live, one deep-tissue massage equals ten bales of hay. My hamstrings grumble after a ten-mile run, but not as loudly as a couple of unfed donkeys. I buy the hay. There's no money left for massages.

Still, I love a good massage when it's free, and I've had three. The first was a gift, a spa day. The second, I won in a raffle.

Then there was Tommy. Tommy, my near-sex experience.

After Tommy, I scoured the Book of Exodus, looking for the lost Eleventh Commandment, but apparently Moses dropped it on the way down the mountain. Here it is:

> *Thou shalt not have a strange man probe and pummel your deep tissues, not whilst thou are married, not whilst thou are single, not whilst thou are breathing and sentient, no matter how sorest thy muscles are.*

Yeah, I broke it.

But, in my defense, I didn't hire Tommy. Tommy was done unto me.

This happened just after the Virginia Beach Half-Marathon, the existence of which threatens to expose one of the most closely guarded secrets of the running world. Think about it: Why are so many of the most popular races held near the ocean? It's not to replenish our salt stores. No, it's one of the greatest scams ever devised, the inconvenience (wink, wink) known as the "out-of-town race."

Tell people you're going to run 13.1 miles in another town, and with enough frowning and sighing in the delivery, you can elicit as much sympathy as if you've told them you're leaving for gum surgery followed by a funeral. Most people can't fathom running thirteen miles, let alone doing it for pleasure, so the idea that you're really off on a hedonistic weekend with a couple of other repressed middle-aged moms doesn't compute. They don't know the race itself just lasts three hours. They have no concept of how much wine will be drunk.

So I'm always up for an out-of-town race, particularly with my friend Christen, who is fitter than me, blonder than me, and can drink everyone I know under the table. Christen is also married to an international pilot, so she can do this while hopscotching through multiple time zones, and while raising two kids, selling real estate, teaching water aerobics, competing in triathlons. You know the type: just your everyday superwoman next door.

You'd hate her, except she's so nice.

So nice that she bought me a massage.

This was when we were living in Richmond. With Virginia Beach less than two hours away, the half-marathon there beckoned, and for the sake of my health, I couldn't say no. Christen and her friend Joan, good sports that they are, drove up from South Carolina so I wouldn't have to run it alone. (Wink, wink.)

The race was hard and tedious, even with excellent company, and afterward I want nothing more than to crash in my hotel room for a nap. But Christen, a stunt double for the Energizer Bunny, is still bopping around, vexingly full of energy, and she decides we all need massages.

"Fine," I say. "You two have fun." On our four-kids/three-firings budget, a massage is a lovely idea but out of the question. Just the race entry and hotel room had been a seriously unjustifiable splurge. Besides, since I love hotels—would live in one if I could—and I'm still aglow with post-race endorphins, it really *is* fine for the two of them to get massages while I nap. We can meet at the Macaroni Grill later.

But no. Christen and Joan have their own post-race endorphins, and theirs are unruly things. They book three massages and pay for mine. Nap be damned, I will be getting a massage at two o'clock whether I want one or not.

Oh, fine.

Grumbling good-naturedly, I climb in Christen's car, and we drive to a squat, gray building that looks suspiciously like a double-wide. Not that I have anything against double-wides, being one myself, but I'm just pointing out that this massage will not be taking place at some hoity Newbury Street address. It's not a massage "parlor" in the sense that the vice squad should be on alert, but I'm not expecting the US Olympic marathoners to be in the back getting their knotty hamstrings untied.

But we're not Olympians, just a few achy moms with too many C-sections among us. It's perfect, really. This will be nice. The pretty brunette receptionist smiles and tells us our massagers will be with us shortly. Christen will have Sarah. Joan will have Suzanne.

I will have Tommy.

Red flag! Red flag! Red flag!

(Dumb blonde! Dumb blonde! Dumb blonde!)

Red flag the size of a Buick? Huh? Where? I'm not seeing it.

Maybe I would, if I were accustomed to getting massages. But at this point, I've had exactly one massage in my life, administered by a woman wearing medical scrubs and sensible shoes, the woman who asked me why, exactly, I wanted the Runner's Revenge. That had not been an experience that would lead me to pay any attention to an assigned massage professional. On the contrary, it taught me to ignore them.

Christen and Joan, however, are more experienced in matters of massage. They exchange glances that I interpret as envy, which troubles me, because they, having paid the bill, ought to be getting the best massagers. Blithely, I offer them Tommy. I'm okay with having Suzanne. Really. Just happy to be here. Just happy to be sitting. You take him.

"Oh no, we're all set!" they say in unison, grinning.

And so, Captain Oblivious here limps down to the hall to my room. There, I strip down to my underwear, wrap a white sheet around me, and hoist myself on the table. The room smells of incense. The music is reminiscent of "Bolero." It throbs. Glumly, I lie down and think of my lost nap and my lovely, empty hotel room. Hotel rooms are so glorious and so ridiculously expensive, I don't see why anyone leaves them for *any* reason. Sometimes I think of getting a job cleaning hotel rooms just so I can hang out in them.

But the wistfulness ends when Tommy comes in. All six-foot-two, 175 well-muscled, deeply tanned pounds of him.

He's half my age. At best. He smiles and asks, throatily, how I am. Mother of God, how did Harry Connick Jr. get in here, and how can I get biceps like that?

Harry masquerading as Tommy the Masseur dims the dim lights even lower. I sit up clumsily, clutching the sheet. I tell him I just ran the marathon. *Half-marathon,* I mean. I am not only a fat runner, but a verbal klutz. But he just nods, fetchingly.

He asks me to lie on my stomach, and tactfully looks away as I flip over and stretch out, the years of excess carbohydrates magically smooshing into the soft surface of the table. Tommy dips his hands in warm lotion, rolls down the sheet, exposes my back, and energetically and shamelessly breaks the little-known but vitally important Eleventh Commandment.

You've heard of the deer in the headlights? I am the deer on the massage table, undressed.

I cannot move. I cannot breathe. I cannot wait to get out of here and strangle Christen and Joan.

I, a mild-mannered, married mother of four, who has never so much as looked at the personals on Craigslist, am practically naked, in a dark room, while a strange man named Tommy is touching me all over.

Worse, he's not just touching. He's kneading me, like a cat. Where's the escape button on this table, the chute that will carry me from this den of perfidy to my chastely decorated hotel room? Shame floods me as Tommy works his way up my legs. You pervert, stay away from my glutes!

But Garrison Keillor is right: Everything becomes appropriate with time. Being massaged while mostly naked by a beautiful man half my age becomes appropriate in, oh, about six minutes.

The horror does not just subside, but turns and bolts out the room, about the time he reaches my left hamstring. It is replaced by a warm and guileless contentment.

It's hard to tell over the throbbing drums keeping pace with Tommy's hands, but I think I am purring. I shall stay here all day.

Then suddenly, in a flash of clarity, I suppress a giggle.

Somewhere in this building, on two tables identical to mine, Christen and Joan are being massaged, too. They think they pulled one on me, getting me assigned to this yeasty young man. I was embarrassed, yes, but only for a few minutes. Now, gorgeously tired, I am being tended to, loved upon, by a young man worthy of Madonna's dance troupe. So what if he had to be paid for the honor? What's a little cash between friends?

I stretch, limp as a drowsy cat, and direct Tommy to a tight muscle. "Here," I say, sighing. "It hurts here. Can you fix it?"

The gift of exertion is not necessarily a long life; even professional athletes can die in their prime. It is, instead, a satisfying intimacy with the bodies we inhabit, a fluidity of movement that a sedentary person cannot comprehend or mimic.

Muscles have memory. They retain information on how to perform tasks without direction from a conscious mind. Our bodies are tools; co-workers, if you will. But, like a colleague eager to share a beer when the workday is done, they, too, can become intimate friends.

Like human friends and lovers, they can be utterly unreliable at times. Cads, even. You can be the closest of friends for a couple of decades, and then awaken one morning and find yourself riddled with cancer. Even if a toenail fungus is the most diseased you ever get, the ultimate betrayal awaits. One day, our bodies will fail every one of us spectacularly, shutting down completely. It's a catastrophic breach of contract that must be forgiven in advance. But forgiving is what friends do.

Tommy fixes my legs, like I have fixed my soul in the sacred act of staggering upright for 13.1 miles. There is a runner's high, yes, but no less significant is the runner's afterglow. It is the delicious exhaustion of a body used to completion. It is the feeling I have now. Spent. Stretched. Limber. Happy. Happy within. Happy without.

Happy without a lot of stuff other people need to be happy.

The test of an experience is not how you feel while you're doing it, but how you feel after it's done. And right now, I'm feeling sublime, thanks to my friend, my body.

I think on these things drowsily as Tommy tucks in my sheet, wishes me a good day, and quietly leaves the room. Reluctantly, I sit up, dress, leave my last twenty on the table, and float down the hall, light as gauze. Christen and Joan are sitting in the lobby, in states of rapture similar to my own. Tommy, Suzanne, Yosemite Sam, whoever. Life is good. We smile at one another and, gloriously limber, head out to the Macaroni Grill.

After a well-earned meal, a couple of bottles of wine, and a good night's sleep, we'll travel back to our homes. There, we'll tell our families how hard the race was, how oozing the blisters, how far away the finish line, how we're never, *ever* doing that again.

Wink, wink.

ten

Roads Scholar

My name is Jennifer, and I am an obsessive-compulsive runner. I've been running now for about ten years.

The green silk dress still hangs in my closet, unworn. I'm no quitter. But I'm starting to think maybe I'll just be buried in it. The undertaker can cut a slit down the back and arrange it loosely around my sides, and no one needs to know it doesn't fit.

Yes, I'm still fat, but that's not to say there haven't been changes. For one thing, the zebra getup is gone. Suffering unfathomable pressure for years, the seams finally surrendered and split open, providing indecent and unwelcome air-conditioning for my inner thighs. For a few weeks, I tried to sew them back to a usable state, but a mile into a run they'd rupture again. So I gave up and ran for a while in a long T-shirt and black clingy capris, the ones I wore to my first Kiawah half.

No, it wasn't a good look. But somewhere I'd gotten the idea that I couldn't run in shorts.

"Somewhere" would be elementary school.

That was when I first became aware of the amazing monkey-like ability of shorts to climb up the legs of fat people. Don't pretend you don't know what I mean.

In any video of a crowd, you can see someone with their shorts sidling up their thighs, like the fabric is seeking higher ground, trying to escape an invisible tsunami. I've spent a lifetime beating down shorts, and I had no intention of doing this while I was out running. Besides, my legs are more dimpled than the Gerber baby's.

But then one day, in a catalog, I saw a pair of running shorts advertised as the "anti-running shorts." These shorts, the ad promised, had a longer inseam than the average pair and were guaranteed not to ride up. Hopeful but suspicious, I ordered a pair: XL, of course, royal blue.

A few days later, the shorts arrived, and when it was time to run I ripped open the package and put them on. They felt okay. They looked okay. The purple Nile that meanders down my right leg was exposed, but whatever. I was going to run down the Washington–Old Dominion bike path near my home in Falls Church, not pose for the cover of *Runner's World*.

Or maybe I *wasn't* going to run the WOD. Maybe I was going to run to the end of the street and then walk back home and change. We'd see.

Tentatively, I trotted a few yards, then more confidently a few dozen. I jogged to the end of my street, turned left at Haycock Elementary, and then, picking up speed and confidence with every stride, ran down the sidewalk toward the trail, courageously facing traffic.

The drivers must have thought I was crazy. *Who is this fat runner grinning so foolishly?*

But the heavens opened. The angels sang.

The shorts did not ride up.

They flapped primly, halfway to my knee. They covered the bulging contour of my hips, and the curdled sludge of chicken gravy molding my derriere.

Gloriously, they let in air. They ventilated like a box fan.

Most important, they made me look—kinda, sorta, maybe—like (dare I say it?) a runner. A fat runner, yes. But a runner.

In my anti-running running shorts, with an iPod on my arm and a water bottle in my hand, no one would ask if I needed a ride.

Probably.

From then on, I ran in shorts whenever it was forty degrees or warmer; in compression tights when it turned cold. What's on my legs, how they feel, I came to realize, is as important as what's on my feet. The feeling—not the reality—makes all the difference.

Within months came another change. I became comfortable running almost anywhere, any time of day.

In the beginning, I'd been rigid as a lamppost, with regular routes, times, and distances from which I didn't deviate. I felt safe in my routines. Using them, I could tell how well I was running. Familiar distances measure progress surely as a ruler.

When I lived on Syrup Mill Road in Blythewood, for example, I knew every pebble on the street, each dip in the pavement, every ding on the stop sign (which I always touched lightly, reverently, like a precious icon, before turning around). I knew it was going to be an excellent run if I got to the second mailbox without gasping, or if I passed the fourth house without slowing. Conversely, if I had to walk before reaching the stop sign, it was not going to be a good day.

For five happy years, I ran up and down that road. In my mind, I was a *part* of it, a permanent feature of the landscape that was just occasionally and necessarily absent.

I conversed cordially with the cows that lived in a pasture two doors down. I collected trash on the side of the road. For a while, until it vanished, I fed a feral kitten I saw in the woods at the end of the street. I'd carry a can of cat food in a plastic bag on my run, stop to empty it on an old plate I left hidden in the weeds, and collect the empty can on the way back home.

My best runs were at night. Since I knew the road so well (and there was rarely snow and ice in the South), I felt comfortable running Syrup Mill Road in the dark. Even my city-loving husband admitted that the country skies were magnificent. Out on the road, in the blackness, the stars applauded my every lumbering step, and every twenty-nine days a creamy full moon lit the way.

But people worried.

My mother and my husband said I'd be killed, if not by a mad stalker, then by a careless driver. Or I'd be a victim of road rage. People sometimes drove too fast on that road, and I'd mutter "Oh, don't mind me" and shake my fist at their retreating taillights.

When a woman was murdered just five miles away, I carried a sharp stick with me until the killer was caught. (As if that would do me any good.) Occasionally, during this time, if a strange car slowed, I felt a ripple of alarm. Mentally, I rehearsed what I would do if a strange man approached, what I would say, where I would run. I tried to never let down my guard. But for the most part, I felt safe. At home. At peace. It was *my* road, after all.

I saw a bumper sticker that said, AS A MATTER OF FACT, I DO OWN THE ROAD.

I wanted one.

Then we moved. My adorable country house had two bedrooms, and our second child was on the way. I didn't want to leave the home that I'd had built when I was single; didn't wanted to leave the dogwood and redbud trees I'd planted; the tiny two-log fireplace; the deck off my bedroom that overlooked quiet woods.

I didn't want to leave the yard in which I'd danced.

The night before we moved, I sat on the front porch, looking out at the road, my road. And cried.

But we'd found a newly restored home in the city, with three bedrooms, four fireplaces, and a fenced yard. It was ten minutes from my office. Like a bowl of bran flakes, it would be good for me . . . eventually.

Putting down new shelf paper in the kitchen the next week, I sat on the kitchen floor, legs crossed, and cried again.

But someone else was now living in my home. I would have to learn to love my new house, find new places to run.

The baby, Alexandra, arrived in September, and after she started sleeping through the night it was time for me to return to the streets. I did so mechanically and joylessly, slowed once again by the baby fat, but this time something else, something unexpected: the unfamiliar streets.

How was I doing? I couldn't tell. On Syrup Mill Road, I knew it was a good day if I made it to the stop sign without slowing. It was a bad day if my side hurt before I saw the cows. The road was my marker, my timekeeper, my companion. Without it, I felt awkward, displaced. My body was heavy, and so was my heart. I missed my road.

So, one day, after mulling it over for a week, I pulled out my sweats, stretched lightly, and climbed into the car. I was going to drive thirty miles to run two miles on my old street.

I'd told Michael what I was doing, since he had to watch the kids, and he'd pronounced it a very bad idea. "You will cry," he predicted. And I knew he might be right. But halfway to Blythewood, I noticed I was singing.

Still, when I saw my beloved street sign, for the first time since we'd moved, I hesitated.

It felt odd, turning down this road, headed toward a house that was no longer mine. *Maybe Michael is right,* I thought. *It's not my road anymore. It's not my neighborhood now. I don't belong here.* But I was here, and I still needed to run.

I parked on the side of the road, on a patch of grass where I used to stop and admire the night sky. I locked the Jeep, hung the key around my neck, and walked to the stop sign. Then, uncertainly, I began a slow lope.

It felt good.

I made it down the street with a minimum of pain—not bad, I thought, for three months postpartum. I didn't cry, as my husband had predicted, but when I touched the stop sign and looked down a road I thought I'd never run again, the air I gulped was poignant.

When I returned home, Michael asked how it went.

"Fine," I said briskly, and that was that. I couldn't convey—and he couldn't have understood—the emotion of that day, that run. Even now, I'm not sure what it meant.

Was it a sign, that little exchange? A sign that Michael and I were fundamentally incompatible? Was I wrong to not try to explain what the road meant to me? Was it wrong that he didn't invest time and sweat trying to understand?

Deeper still: Can a town mouse truly love a country mouse? *Green Acres* was just a silly 1960s sitcom. Who knows if Eva and Eddie could have reconciled the chores and the stores in real life? What makes for thigh-slapping comedy on television can make for existential angst in a marriage.

But we had two children under the age of three, and in the frolicking din of two-career domesticity, such questions went unrecognized and undebated.

But I returned to Blythewood again. And again.

For several months, until I was comfortably entrenched in a running routine again, I returned to Syrup Mill Road every Sunday.

I still ran during the week in the city, on sidewalks pockmarked with holes. I didn't like it, but it was necessary, or else my Sunday run would be unpleasant and hard.

There's something else, though.

When I ran on Syrup Mill Road when I lived in the city, I didn't run the whole way. I'd always stop and turn around before I got to my little house and the front porch where I used to collapse, panting.

The house, after all, was no longer mine, and I'd come to accept that.

The house wasn't mine and wouldn't be again. But hey, I do own the road.

eleven

Please Come to Boston

I've never stopped missing my little house in Blythewood. I still dream about it, once even tried to buy it again, even though I now live in another cool house. This one was modeled after the farmhouse on the TV show *Bonanza,* but that's not the cool part.

The cool part is where it is: in Hopkinton, Massachusetts, the Holy Grail of real estate for runners.

We moved here because . . . drumroll . . . Michael was fired once again, although again, he was fired up the ladder. Generally speaking, you can't go wrong opposing the Council of American-Islamic Relations, at least not in the post-9/11 world. So this time, Michael not only got multiple job offers but signed with a big-name agent, to boot. And having an agent meant something resembling job security in a famously volatile profession.

It meant, finally, we could a buy a house.

We'd been renting since we left Charlotte, too broke and too scared to take a chance on buying again. But Boston was looking like home. Boston was TFD.

TFD meant "the final destination." This was written in black Sharpie on a dozen or so sealed boxes stuffed in closets and under beds. We'd been moving them around for years. They contained books and trinkets and furnishings we wanted to keep, but could never unpack because there was no room in our cramped rentals.

In Boston, we'd finally get to unpack the TFDs.

Even though it was going to be a two-day drive to visit my parents and my grandmother, there were other reasons I was excited about moving to Boston. Full of history and charm, it's a lot like Charleston, just colder. It has four seasons, fresh lobster, and Cambridge, and Walden Pond, and Concord's Minuteman Bikeway, and . . . of course, the greatest road race in the world.

When we first looked at our soon-to-be-home, the real estate agent said, apologetically, "The only problem with Hopkinton is that the Boston Marathon starts here, and a lot of people hate all the roads being closed, and all the noise and hoopla."

"Sold!" I said, wondering what kind of closed-minded, sedentary rube would consider this a problem.

"It All Starts Here!" is the motto of Hopkinton, and the marathon course passes not just one spot on my street, but three. That makes three glorious spaces where my kids and I can gather each April for front-row viewing of one of the greatest athletic contests in the world, for free. Honestly, they should charge extra for the privilege of living here. Not only do I get to see the world's greatest athletes run by my street, but sometimes they take off their pants.

True story: Every year, my neighbors and I congregate at the end of our street to cheer on the parade of runners. We are there from the first press car to the last juggling bandit, three-plus hours on our feet. One of my neighbors brings hot dogs and beer, and yells, "That's what I'm talking about!" every time an especially pretty marathoner runs by.

Our usual spot is near the one-mile marker, where runners shed their throwaway clothes—the ratty sweats and old T-shirts they wear to stay warm in the chilly hours before the start.

One year, my neighbor Bob and I were standing together, clapping until our palms were chapped, when a female runner darted out of the pack, stood next to us, and peeled off her long black pants to reveal nylon shorts underneath. "My address and five dollars are in the pocket; these are my favorite pants," she said. "Would you please mail them back to me?"

Would we? Heck yes! Bob and I, we were so proud.

Some runners say crowds are important, but in truth, spectators on a marathon course are a lowly lot. Especially if you're a spectator who runs.

With thousands of triumphant runners streaming past you, living their dreams, it's easy to feel insignificant if you're just standing there clapping. When a runner thanks you for being there, or slaps your outstretched hand, it takes away some of the sting.

But when a runner takes off her pants and gives them to you, it's potentially a life-changing event.

So we took the pants, and the marathoner ran off, and Bob and I stood there proudly, newly endowed with a sense of duty and purpose. We spent the rest of the race arguing about who would assume the task of packaging and mailing the pants.

Bob won, me having the hindrance of multiple small kids. It was okay. Bob is an internationally known and respected engineer. He's a veteran. He's from Vermont. The kind of man you know you can trust. I knew he'd take good care of the pants.

But a few weeks later, when I ran past him out working in his yard,

Bob raised a hand and motioned me over. "We've got a problem," he said. "There was five dollars in the pocket, but no address. I have no way to mail that lady her pants."

We decided the slip of paper must have fallen out when she took off the pants and was forever lost in the damp sludge of smashed paper cups. Bob felt badly about it all, but not so much that he couldn't spend the five on a double-shot espresso at Dunkin' Donuts. He was planning to drop off the pants at the local Goodwill.

I was aghast.

"Those were her favorite pants! You can't do that! You give them to me!" I scolded him until he gave in.

I took the pants home and looked at them longingly. They were medium Asics, too small for me, but so soft and comfortable. Maybe, if I start a diet tomorrow, they might fit me in a couple of months.

Yeah, right. They'll fit me just as well as the green silk dress.

My own tenuous grasp on reality aside, the incident revealed the great divide: the yawning, unleapable chasm between those who run and those who won't.

Bob, you see, is not a runner. He walks, but that's not the same.

Runners—*especially* fat runners—know that a favorite pair of pants, or shorts, or a faded old race T-shirt, is not something you can easily replace at the spring sale at the Sports Authority. There are some articles of clothing, broken in by blood, sweat, and years, that make us faster, stronger, thinner. A zebra-striped, turquoise warm-up suit, for example.

That woman needed her pants. I swore a solemn oath to reunite them.

Over the next few months, I composed an essay about the mystery woman and her lost pants, and pitched it, first to *The Boston Globe* (which occasionally publishes my musings, but providentially declined this tale), and then to *Runner's World* magazine.

When I connected with Katie Neitz, an editor at *Runner's World* at the time, she was working on a Boston Marathon–themed edition and just happened to have some space.

Coincidence, they say, is just God's way of remaining anonymous.

And so, a few months later, all the way across the country, in San Diego, it came to pass that a professor of exercise physiology was thumbing through her new issue of *Runner's World* and stumbled across an artist's rendition of her long-lost pants. She called *Runner's World,* and they gave her my phone number.

"Mo-om," Galen yelled when she called that night. "The pants lady is on the phone."

Poor Laura will now forever go by that name.

The pants and pants lady were joyfully reunited at the next Boston Marathon expo, at a meet-up arranged and filmed by *Runner's World,* which published a follow-up article the next month. Laura and I are doomed to obscurity now, since that weekend, we used up every one of our fifteen minutes of fame. The local TV stations filmed me handing the pants to Laura. *Runner's World* interviewed each of us, separately and together, for a lengthy video on the magazine's website. Never before has a single pair of pants gotten so much press.

I made my highly bored children go with me to the expo, because I wanted them to see that their mother, like their father, occasionally made news, if only by the act of standing by the side of the road, clapping.

Later that night, my mother called. She had news. My perfect, thin, beautiful cousin Stephanie and her perfect, thin, beautiful husband were divorcing.

I was stunned. Her life, her marriage, her thighs, always seemed so perfect to me.

Stephanie had two young children, close in age to mine: a boy and girl, both beautiful, both thin. My children, while not fat like I was, like I'd been, always looked a husk away from corn-fed.

I was sorry for the sake of the children, but there was a small, guilty part of me that, despicably, relished this news. Schadenfreude, they call it. In German, pleasure at the misfortune of others.

In English: Misery loves company.

And I've got so much misery here. If every married couple south of Virginia divorced, it wouldn't be company enough.

The next day, I went to Hopkinton Drug to look for a card to send Stephanie. I didn't want to call and ask probing questions, but I felt the need to reach out. We've never been close—separated by ten years and, at any given time, fifty to seventy-five pounds—but we're first cousins and only children, and she's the closest thing to a peer in my immediate family.

One thing I've never understood: why, in a nation with a divorce rate hovering around 50 percent, there are hundreds of anniversary cards, but hardly any divorce cards. There were exactly two divorce cards at Hopkinton Drug. Both were celebratory. For the mother of young children, that didn't seem right.

For *anybody*, that doesn't seem right.

I gave up, but on my way out, passed by the store's small selection of wedding and shower gifts. There, among the silver frames and crystal candlesticks, I spotted a coffee mug and dishtowel with one of those feisty 1950s housewives and the words, WHY DO I HAVE TO GET MARRIED? I DIDN'T DO ANYTHING WRONG.

The blond woman on the dishtowel looked exactly like my mother in her wedding pictures, forty-five years ago.

I bought three. One for Stephanie . . . my mother . . . and me.

twelve

Speed Goggles

My ex-husband didn't run.

Well, okay, maybe I should have delved into my separation and divorce before now, but frankly, all that mess—and in the last few years, it was a colossal, oozing, infected, inflamed, supermassive bunion of a mess—had little to do with my running.

Throughout our eighteen-year marriage, Michael's primary role in my running career was to watch the kids and occasionally finance new running shoes and a drawer full of blister-free socks.

I'd been running nearly five years by the time Michael and I got married. He hated running, hated it ever since he had to run laps for his high school basketball team. If I'd begged him, I suppose he would have joined me, but I didn't beg, and he didn't ask. We did walk together on Syrup Mill Road when I was nine months' pregnant, but mostly so he could push me up the hills.

Later, as our marriage was imploding and we were rolling through a string of ineffective counselors, I remarked in a therapy session that it seemed like a bad thing for your life partner to have so little interest in such a big part of your life.

"But you don't want me to run with you," Michael protested. "You like to run alone."

Well, yes. That was true, much of the time. The loneliness—and the loner-ness—of the long-distance runner is well documented in book and in film.

But it was also true that, occasionally, I wished he had been there when a deer bounded across my path, or when a dolphin sprang up in the water and paralleled my run down the beach, or when, running through a forest thirty miles from the city, I happened upon an unexpected and extraordinary skyline of Boston.

I would have liked to have shared these things, and my various foot ailments. I earnestly wished he had hammertoes, too.

But Michael was not there on my runs, nor at my finish lines. It became a running gag—literally and figuratively—what was going to keep him and the kids away when I finished a race. Sometimes they overestimated my time; other times, it was traffic. Although I've been a parent for nineteen years, and raced for more than a decade, I have yet to experience seeing my children cheering me at the finish line, or holding a GO MOMMY GO! sign meant for me.

It was tough, I know. Four kids are a load. And he did watch them so I could race. I knew and appreciated that.

I resigned myself. At the end of the Kiawah Island Half-Marathon, they have this amazing bean soup that's almost as good as a GO MOMMY GO! sign.

Okay.

Everyone wants to know what happened when people divorce, so they can assure themselves it won't happen to them.

Let me just say that, unless your husband happens to be a talk-radio host whose weapon of choice is mockery, and you happen to be a fat runner with four kids who probably, let's be honest, should *not* have been a stay-at-home mom, then no, what happened to me probably won't happen to you. You're safe.

But you probably should stay off the Internet.

The reasons my marriage blew up are dark and dense. My truth is not my ex-husband's truth, and that was the core of the mess. Since we could never agree on what our problems were, we could never find a solution.

We both did reprehensible things.

My reprehensible thing was that I became good friends—far too good a friend than a married woman should be—with a man who revered my running. Someone who not only wanted to run with me, but who wanted to clock me with his stopwatch. Someone who remembered my times in every race. Someone who analyzed all my splits.

It started out benign, as these sorts of things almost always do. An email in response to something I'd written. A polite response. Another email. Another response.

If anyone ever conducts a survey of inappropriate relationships begun on the Internet, I'm pretty sure most will involve southerners, because there's no way any woman raised in the South is going to be the first one to end a conversation. That's just not how we do it down south.

And so it went. An email. A response. An IM.

He lived far away. We would never meet. There were no flashing red lights.

They say every snowflake in an avalanche pleads not guilty.

We became friends. People knew we were friends. He became friends with my friends. He passed through my town, a couple of times, on business. We went to lunch. Another email. Still, there were no flashing red lights.

None that I noticed, anyway.

But one day, we woke up and were too-good-a-friends. Enough that it was affecting my marriage.

Please know: We did not violate the Seventh Commandment, but we played fast and loose with the Tenth. I am not proud of this. I am deeply ashamed of it, just like I'm deeply ashamed of my back fat.

I am not ashamed of *him,* of having gotten to know this brilliant, sensitive, and extraordinarily capable human being. Just the ugly, misshapen, and highly flammable thing we so blithely made.

There it is. My reprehensible thing.

You'll have to ask my former husband about his.

I didn't realize the damage I was doing to my marriage until one day when I read an essay in *Running Times* magazine titled "Speed Goggles: Why Fast Men Make the Heart Beat Quicker." In it, Rachel Toor wrote about her frustrating search for a STYF man.

STYF: smarter, taller, younger, and faster.

"Speed goggles" was Toor's riff on "beer goggles"—the description of how your vision gets warped when you look at the world through those things.

"I know lots of great and handsome men who slog through marathons at a slow and steady pace," she wrote. "It's not that I wouldn't go out with them, but when I see the cadaverous guys striding out before the gun goes off, my heart begins to race."

I got that. I so got that.

I would never want a *cadaverous* guy—if I accidentally rolled over on him during the night, I might kill him—but I understood Toor's longing for an athletic man who matched her in ability or, at the very least, challenged her and admired her stride.

Of course, there was a fundamental problem here. Toor was single. I was married.

When I looked through speed goggles at my sedentary husband, as much as I loved him, he was unpreventably diminished. I knew this, and tried not to use those goggles, but sometimes they seemed stuck there, glued to me. Like the ocean, they were an agent of erosion.

There was also another problem, a minor thing, but a significant communication gap between a runner and a non-running spouse: The non-runners don't know the right questions to ask.

"How was your run?" Michael would ask perfunctorily when I staggered, dripping and red-faced, through the door.

Sometimes I would answer "great"—other times, I'd say "painful"—and that would be the end of the discussion, just like when I returned from running on Syrup Mill Road for the first time after we'd moved.

Since my husband didn't run, he couldn't know the questions I longed to answer, the questions that would have led to greater intimacy. He didn't know to ask what I saw on my run, or if anything was aching and needed a rub, or what I was listening to on my iPod that day on my run, or if I'd noticed that the moon was out already at the end of our road even though it was just 4 PM.

And I never offered any of these things, not only because I didn't really want him to know that I'd just run for forty-one minutes listening to an endless loop of Nickleback on my iPod (I swear, my teenage daughter put it there), but because as a non-runner, I knew he could never relate. Nor would he ever ask the questions I wanted to hear, and wanted to answer: How far did you run? And, how fast?

Only another runner would ask those questions and really care about what the answer would be.

Speed goggles. My husband lacked speed goggles.

But what the hell. I lacked speed.

thirteen

Everyone Has Their Daimons

I talk to dead people.

Oh, come on. Name me one interesting person who doesn't.

Hillary Clinton was ridiculed for revealing that she has inner conversations with Eleanor Roosevelt. But there are 2.2 billion Catholics in this world who pray (that is, *talk*) to the saints, and the first requirement for sainthood, last time I checked, is extinction.

Anyone who doesn't occasionally converse with the dead is, in my opinion, either lying or uninspired.

Me, I talk to Steve Prefontaine. And, look away if this pains you, but occasionally, yeah, he talks back.

You might think this began in the roiling, panicky pain of my separation and divorce, but no. It started a few years earlier, when I decided I needed a coach. It's all the rage, you know. The US Department of Labor reports that the number of personal trainers doubled last year, and the field is going to grow in double digits for at least the next decade. Everybody who is serious about running, it seems, has some sort of coach, even if only online.

It's the nature of the sport.

Running, you see, is unique among sports in that everyone who wants to gets to play. Except for, say, the Olympics, and invitational track meets, it's all comers, all the time. This is not true of other sports.

You may love football and block like a six-hundred-pound mule, but no matter how good you are in your backyard at the biannual family reunion, you can't show up at the Super Bowl and trot out on the field with the Patriots.

You can, however—if you're a half-decent runner—register for Boston, or the New York City Marathon, and race the same course as Ryan Hall, Meb Keflezighi, and the world's elite runners. You can trot your endomorph self down the road right behind them.

Not, of course, that you'd ever catch up.

But to us road runners, that doesn't matter. Long-distance running, for the masses, is the ultimate contest of man-against-self. It doesn't matter if we don't have legs like Olympian Galen Rupp, or a coach like famed marathoner Alberto Salazar. For a while, we take our rightful place in the back of the pack and are happy with that.

But then—egad!—we improve. Maybe not a lot. Maybe just a little.

It only takes a little.

We run a 5K; we want to run a 10K. We run a 10K; we want to run a half-marathon. We run a half-marathon; we start dreaming about a full.

The Boston Marathon accepts about twenty-seven thousand runners each year. Most of them pay the $150 registration fee, and train for a year or more, to start in the second or third wave of runners, thirty or forty minutes after the top contenders begin. Some take seven hours to finish. Few, if any, regret it.

It's heady stuff, running the streets of Boston, where a hundred thousand spectators turn out to cheer as you huff by. It is a gauntlet of adulation, and after a while, as they say, you start to believe your own press. *Hey, maybe I am hot stuff. I've got potential. Maybe all I need is a better pair of shoes, and another ten miles a week, and a few tweaks to my diet, and I could start up at the front with Lance. Maybe a coach . . . yeah, that's all I need is a coach!*

Writer Anne Lamott says the truth always bats last, and here it steps up to the plate.

There is something mildly ludicrous—nay, hugely ludicrous—about the personal-trainer craze. Between the Internet, libraries, and bookstores, there is no scrap of information about the training of athletes that is not available—*for free*—to us all.

Alberto Salazar may be a very good coach, and he has won many races and trained many top runners. But he's training people to *run,* something any neurologically typical two-year-old can do.

Even the late great Bill Bowerman said, "Stress . . . recover . . . improve. That's all training is. You'd think any damn fool could do it."

The average person needs assistance to master, say, physics. We need not spend vast sums of money to learn how to *run* better.

That said, yes, I, too, wanted a coach.

One day, I'd had this idea: What if you took a middle-aged hack runner—oh, for the sake of conversation, let's say *me*—with no great physical gifts, no history of athleticism, and a plethora of varicose veins and loyal-to-the-death cellulite, and paired her with a coach of some repute? What improvements might occur? (Or, perhaps more likely, what hilarity might ensue?)

I knew that, as an ordinary stay-at-home mother, my chances of finding a top-level coach (for no money) were practically nil. But, I thought, if I approached this as a reporter, maybe I could find someone with just enough ego to bite.

So I composed this letter. It's verbatim, as I sent it out.

Dear Alberto Salazar:

An athlete of your stature is constantly awash in invitations and appeals for assistance, so I apologize in advance for adding to the demands on your time.

I am a freelance journalist and a recreational runner, not always in that order. For several years, I've been mulling an idea that I think has potential: What would happen if you paired an elite coach with a middle-aged mom? Could an acclaimed coach, someone who trains young and naturally gifted athletes, also succeed with someone not-so-young and not-so-gifted? Are the limits of the human body set by the mind, the body, or are they false boundaries that reflect merely the dearth of an able coach?

Could an athlete/coach of your caliber take someone like me— a thick-thighed mother of four, who is not a natural athlete, and never competed as a youth—into an athlete who could win, or at least be competitive, in a road race in my age group?

I don't know. And neither do you. Care to find out with me?

Full disclosure: You wouldn't have much to work with. I am no Joan Benoit Samuelson. I have struggled with weight all my life, and run 11- and 12-minute miles. I have been running for more than 15 years, with no marked improvement in my mileage or times. I have occasional tightness in my left knee, but am fundamentally healthy and sound, and, other than a bout of bursitis 10 years ago, have never had any running-related injuries. I run 5K races a few times a year, and a half-marathon every now

and then. My last half-marathon time was—don't laugh—2:16,
and I was ecstatic with that.

If you would consider this venture and agree to talk further,
please give me a call. Thank you so much for your time and con-
sideration.

Nice, huh? Polite, respectful, sycophantic—I'm from the South,
you know.

For two years, while I was still married, I sent variations of this
letter out, to a handful of the top US running coaches. No response.
Not a note, not a call, not a nibble.

A more reasonable person would have stopped after a month, since
looming in my empty mailbox was the potential for a soul-crushing
loss of self-esteem. Remember, because of my various fat-childhood
torments, I don't suffer rejection well.

But this was different. I knew this was a good idea. To hell with
Alberto Salazar. Really, how much trouble would it have been to ask
his secretary to compose an email saying, "I'm so sorry, but you're
too insignificant for me"?

So instead, I signed on with Steve Prefontaine.

Who died in 1975.

This is not as odd as it sounds, since I'd been talking to my hero
George Sheehan for a couple of years, and he died in 1993.

Prefontaine, an Olympian and long-distance running legend, famously smashed his sports car into a rock when I was twelve, long before I was cognizant of him. But I actually met Dr. Sheehan.

He was a New Jersey cardiologist who took up running in his forties and forged a new career writing about the existential aspects of
the sport. I first came across him at the library the week after I

dreamed about running around Lake Katherine. I checked out *Running and Being* and renewed it three times. It didn't teach me how to run—I'd have to figure that out myself—but it spoke to me in a way that no how-to manual ever could. It became, for me, a secular bible.

Dr. Sheehan believed a human being cannot achieve his mental and spiritual potential unless he also fulfills his potential as an athlete. A vigorous body leads to a vigorous mind.

"First, be a good animal," his beloved Emerson had said, and Dr. Sheehan engaged his animal self by pushing his body and listening carefully to its whispered revelations. But no matter how hard he ran, how hard he pushed, to Dr. Sheehan, running was fundamentally about play.

"If you would not age, you must make everything you do touched with play, play of the body, of thought, of emotions. If you do, you will belong to that special class of people who find joy and happiness in every act, in every moment," he wrote in *Running and Being*.

My hometown, Columbia, puts on a marathon, and in 1992 Dr. Sheehan was invited to speak at the pre-race symposium. Learning this, I was delirious with joy, the kind of joy a border collie might have if he woke up in a giant, greasy vat of bacon.

But there was a problem. At the time, I was a religion writer for *The State*, Columbia's morning newspaper.

The press conference would be open to sportswriters only. But I quickly figured out a way around that.

Sport as religion. Of course.

Sheehan, deeply spiritual and Catholic, often wrote of the connection himself. Heck, his work was practically theology. "God loves runners," he wrote, "who refuse to quit on hills."

I submitted my request. Score!

Dr. Sheehan, I was told, would see me at three.

Not only did I get into the press conference, quaking in adulation, but I got to ask him a few questions privately afterward. When I told him I run regularly, he didn't laugh. Didn't even look puzzled. He invited me to the symposium, even got me a seat up front.

That night, beginning his talk, Dr. Sheehan mentioned the religion writer in the front row, a chest-swelling point of pride that I recorded. That tape (after my children and my stick of Bodyglide) is the first thing I will grab if the house catches on fire.

Over the years, I'd bought all of Dr. Sheehan's books. There were many. *Running to Win. Personal Best. Going the Distance. This Running Life. Dr. Sheehan on Running. Dr. Sheehan's Medical Advice for Runners. How to Feel Great 24 Hours a Day.*

He also wrote a monthly column for *Runner's World* magazine. He was a one-man publishing house, until he died of cancer in 1993, a little more than a year after we met.

Still, though, he continued to speak to me.

Have you ever read so much of an author that you start to talk, or think, in her voice? Example: When I'm reading Emily Brontë's *Wuthering Heights,* I don't hurry. I hasten. I don't ask. I entreat. The author's language washes over me, like water, and is slow to leave.

Even the Bible has that effect on me. Ten minutes with St. Luke, and it's "verily, verily" for me the rest of the day.

Likewise, I spent so much time reading Dr. Sheehan that I started to think like him. I didn't need a wristband that said WHAT WOULD GEORGE SHEEHAN DO? For the answer, I only needed to turn inward to the channel in my brain where he was broadcasting twenty-four seven.

Of course, in real life, such familiarity would have been a horrific turn of events for us both. Like me, he was fundamentally a loner who needed large amounts of solitude. I am this way because I was an only child. He said he was a loner because he was an ectomorph.

I think it's more likely because he and his wife had twelve kids.

"I find no happiness in carnival, no joy in community," he wrote. Yeah. Twelve kids are a load.

"To read George Sheehan is not necessarily to like him" is how I started my column.

"This is, after all, the man who, like Emerson, likes man but dislikes men; who prefers his own company to almost anyone else's, who writes unabashedly about his selfishness, his forgetfulness, his total self-absorption. He writes, about going to a party, 'I usually wander into the kitchen for a cup of coffee, then find a large book and a quiet place to read until the festivities are over.'"

But that was before he died. After his passing, he seemed much more social, more willing to put the book down and talk. Frequently, he'd open a window in my frontal lobe and bellow something encouraging across the void there.

As the years went by, though, I found my stride, and his books moved from my nightstand to the living room bookshelf. My running became more of a perfunctory thing—dare I say, a habit? I pounded my miles out without needing instruction. I read him less, heard him less. Until the day he introduced me to Steve Roland Prefontaine.

Stay with me here.

I have not recently, nor have I ever, attended a séance or visited a fortune-teller or had my tarot cards read in some seedy portion of town. (Although, full disclosure: I did once own an Ouija board as a child.)

I do not believe in ghosts, or even reincarnation, for that matter. I think if Harry Houdini could have come back, he would have, and it would have been on *Drudge Report.*

But, when I am quiet inside, when I plunge through the outer layers of chaos that rule my noisy, child-infested daily life, there is a place deep inside of serenity and calm. Oddly enough, it seems to be double occupancy. There's more than one voice in this quiet, soothing place, and it is distinctly different from mine.

It's not the same as the peripheral voices in my head, such as that of my former husband, with whom I still argue voraciously every day. Nor is it a remembered voice, like that of my late beloved grandfather.

It could be God, or angels, or devils, or simply my left brain conversing with my right. It could be my higher self and my lower self. My ego and my soul.

Or, hell, for all I know, it could be the long-dead George Sheehan. Not even Darwin could prove that it's not.

So it came to pass that, one November, while struggling up a hill in West Virginia, I sensed not just one presence besides me, but two: a kind, craggy doctor, long departed this Earth, accompanied by a contemptuous rube.

"Rube" was the nickname given to Prefontaine by his coach, Bill Bowerman, who is now immortalized on the inserts of my Nike+ running shoes. It means someone awkward and unsophisticated. Some might say someone like me.

"Here she is," my hero George Sheehan was saying to Pre, who was clearly not happy to be here. "She's no Olympian, but, for her size, she works just as hard as you did."

Now, I am a psychological freak of nature, a hermit who likes an audience. I do everything better if someone is watching me. (Okay, everything except for sex; guys, please don't get any ideas.)

But seriously, doesn't everyone? Aren't the dishes a little bit cleaner if your mother-in-law is watching you do them? Your lines straighter if the neighbor is looking over the fence while you cut grass?

Same thing on the run.

If someone is watching me—whether it's the Weston Nurseries crew looking up curiously as I run by, or, say, a couple of dead guys on a mountain—I tend to straighten my shoulders and lengthen my stride, pick the pace up just a little.

I struggled harder. No way was I going to stop and walk now. I was rounding a curve leading to a sharp incline more tortuous than any road I ever ran in Boston. I trotted up it resolutely.

Pre was unimpressed. I'm pretty sure he smirked.

"No, listen to me, she's got potential," Dr. Sheehan insisted. "I've been helping her with her breathing, but you can help her learn to run faster."

He didn't reply.

Or maybe he did, and my death rattle drowned him out.

Up and down the hills I flailed, seven miles in all. Not once did I engage with the surly figure watching me in my head. I sensed derision, and I've had enough of that in my life. I've been thinking of buying a sign I saw recently that said BE NICE OR LEAVE.

But I was grateful anew for the good doctor, a kindly man. I didn't know why he was dragging this arrogant Olympian into my life, but I knew that, like the government, he was there to help.

Probably.

"You don't have to decide today," Dr. Sheehan said to Prefontaine. "You just keep watching her for now."

I am an only child; a loner. Like most only children, when I was young, I had a stable of imaginary friends.

But suddenly I find myself, approaching midlife and almost certain dementia, on the verge of acquiring an imaginary coach.

Worse, an imaginary coach with an attitude. Alberto Salazar couldn't have disdained me more.

Maybe I am cracking up. My emotional life is in shambles. My youngest daughter kissed my face one day and said I tasted like the ocean.

It was salt, of course. Salt from the ever-present tears damming up my pores. If they're not dripping down my face, they're swelling up behind my eyes.

Where is the anteroom for tears, anyway? They're so hot. I wish, in winter, they could be stored in my hands or my feet, where the little tear heater could actually do me some good.

Angry tears seem hotter than sad tears. Happy tears are cold. I am an authority on the temperature of tears. I am a tear factory. I leak unhappiness.

My former husband has a girlfriend.

I haven't met her, but his grandmother tells me she is thirty-three. Jesus's age when he died. Michael once wrote that by the age of thirty-three, people ought to have done something significant with their lives. Written a book, split the atom, died on a cross to save the world.

I wonder what her significant thing is.

When I was thirty-three—this was a long time ago—Michael did-n't think I had one. Once, in an argument soon after I'd given birth to our second child, he'd spit at me, "What have *you* ever done with your life?"

Oh, hell, I dunno. Created a couple of new human beings?

But I do know what I am going to do with my life this year. Run another half-marathon.

It's been ten years since I first ran Kiawah. My life today bears no resemblance to my life back then.

Except, of course, for my lumpy old body. Even though I've been on a diet, or starting one tomorrow, for the entire decade, my body is essentially the same.

Or is it?

Seems as good a time as any to find out.

A lot of people my size run marathons for somebody—the Leukemia Association, the Cancer Society, a close relative who passed away. Me, I think I'll run it for thirty-three-year-olds. I want to beat every damn one of them in this race.

Prefontaine? You there?

I'm thinking I might need a coach.

PART TWO

"Suppose we have only dreamed, or made up, all those things—trees and grass and sun and moon and stars and Aslan himself. Suppose we have. Then all I can say is that, in that case, the made-up things seem a good deal more important than the real ones."
—C. S. Lewis, The Silver Chair

fourteen

Incriminating Hoofprints

I am riding a bike, rather ungracefully, with a man who is not my husband, and my husband—okay, dammit, *ex*-husband—is off, God-knows-where, with a woman who is not his wife.

Not yet, anyway.

My repeated attempts to reconcile have been as effective as my thirty-year diet, which is to say, I'm still divorced and I'm still fat, even though I run a gazillion or so miles every week. And now, of course, my former husband has gone and found himself a younger, thinner woman, and when a man does that, really, what can you do?

Not that any of this matters right now.

Right now, all that matters is that I get home before the school bus does, and so Sam and I are pumping it, pedaling our bikes as fast as my aching calves will allow.

Normally, I'd already be out on the porch, drinking coffee while I wait for the kids. But Sam has come over to help me fix a few things around the house, and after that, the New England autumn seduces us. The trees that were so stately and dignified in the spring have morphed overnight into hussies. Soon they will shamelessly shed their leaves, but for a few more days they remain maples without morals, flaming exhibitionists putting on a show.

On a day like this, Sam and I agree, you have to be outside or your soul starts to ache, and frankly, I don't need any other parts of me hurting. So we ride our bikes to the local turkey farm, where we eat lunch outside on an old wooden picnic table, picking through a couple of turkey-salad wraps and the respective ruins of our lives.

This takes a while, longer than I was expecting. So now, we have just twenty minutes to pedal four miles back to my house before the first of my kids get home. I am panting from exertion, but we're almost there.

Up ahead is the stop sign where we will part. He will turn left and cycle a mile to his car, parked at Weston Nurseries because it's too soon after the divorce to be introducing a new man to my kids.

I will turn right and coast two hundred yards to my house, where I will wheel the bike into the barn and sprint to the Adirondack chair where I wait each afternoon for the kids. Perfect timing.

Except the donkeys are in the road.

As I turn, I see them coming, my insurance agent's worst nightmare. They are a hundred yards away, galloping straight toward me: fur flying, nostrils flared, hooves clattering on uneven pavement. Foggy is first, leading the charge; his loyal girlfriend, Jo-Jo, a few feet behind him. Together, they are 850 pounds of runaway donkey. They're not even bothering to stay in their lane.

As if on cue, I hear a couple of cars coming up behind them.

I freeze.

Wasn't there a scene like this in *Pet Sematary*? Something in the road, then a rumble, then a Micmac burying ground, and ultimately, nothing good ever happens again in what little bit of life you have left.

Panicking, I unclip my shoes from the bike pedals, hop off, and pitch the bike to the side of the road. Assessing the situation, I come to this conclusion: I need help.

Even more help than I've needed in the past three horrible years.

Oh dear God and Mother Mary—and Moses, too, if you happen to be listening—I need policemen, and roadblocks, and an ambulance, and a horse trailer, and a jug of Merlot, some Krispy Kreme doughnuts, and a large-animal vet with a tranquilizer gun.

But the only help around is on his bike, heading the opposite way.

I turn and shriek, *"Donkeys! Donkeys in the road!"* hoping Sam will hear me, forget the agreed-upon necessity of hiding from my kids, and speed back to rescue me and my unusually long-eared pets. But all I see is the back of his blue-jean jacket, enveloping his hunched-over shoulders, as he pedals away, obliviously, calmly, back to his livestock-free car.

Moses would be more useful to me at this point.

I turn back to the furry problems at hand.

The donkeys are almost upon me, and, because things can *always* get worse—don't let anyone tell you otherwise—I realize they are not wearing their halters. This means, even if they careened to a halt right in front of me and brayed enthusiastically, "Mom! Where ya been?" I'd still have no way to catch them and lead them back home.

No matter what tales you've heard out of Bethlehem, donkeys don't generally tag alongside you, like a small child or a dog. Without a halter, Foggy goes where *he* wants to, which, right now, clearly is not home.

But that oncoming-train-of-a-dilemma can wait. Right now I don't need to get them *home,* just off the road before they cause a ten-car/two-donkey pileup that will lead on CNN.

Thanks be to Moses, the first car on the scene stops. I can't see the driver, so I don't know if he is amused or irate, but at least he can see what is happening. The drivers behind him can't, and so, predictably—this being the North and all—someone leans on his horn.

This is bad, very bad. Foggy hates horns. They scare him.

Everything scares Foggy. Plastic bags, rustling leaves, birds, garbage cans, the wind, the farrier, the vet, the mailman, chipmunks, pinecones, the rate of inflation, and the neighbor's children.

I have no time to work on my crippling emotional issues because I spend so much time trying to fix Foggy's crippling emotional issues, which prevent him from being a good riding donkey, or a good Nativity-scene donkey, or a good donkey for anything at all. And believe me, there's nothing quite so useless as a cowardly donkey in an industrialized nation.

But right now I'm the one who is scared. Foggy's having the time of his life.

I stand there helplessly in the intersection and wave my hands in the air like a rookie police officer in a traffic jam, although I'm pretty sure Foggy and Jo-Jo have no respect for hand signals.

"Stop, donkeys, stop!" I yell, dimly aware of how stupid this sounds.

Then a horrible thought comes to me. I am going to die here, run over by donkeys, surrounded by irate motorists, while the man who is not my husband pedals blithely away. A young, thin woman is going to raise my children and send the donkeys off to auction: Jo-Jo and Foggy, coming soon to a can of Alpo near you.

And dammit, I'm never going to know what it's like to stand on a bathroom scale and not cringe.

How did I get here, to this chaotic intersection? More important, how do I get out?

I close my eyes. Should I click my heels together three times? Cross myself? The donkeys are closing in. Jo-Jo is so close, I can see her drooling.

And then I hear a rumbling behind me, the screech of aging brakes.

There is a God, and he has a sick sense of humor. It's the school bus, right on time.

Have I mentioned Foggy is scared of school buses?

I steel myself to meet my fate, realizing that sometimes, even if you've done everything right, even if you lock the barn securely and double-check the stall bolts and inspect the fencing each week, disaster comes for you anyway.

Nobody knows this better than my new buddy, Steve Roland Prefontaine.

fifteen

Blood, Sweat, and Jeers

We survived Donkeygeddon. There was only one casualty.

My teenagers, mercifully, had not been on the bus. They'd stayed after school for football practice and drama rehearsal.

And help arrived. Not Moses, not an ambulance, but an experienced horsewoman driving a pickup truck. Sensing imminent disaster—equestrians have a special nose for this—she pulled to the side of the road, hopped out, and ran by the bus to help.

Meanwhile, a neighbor who lives near the intersection heard the clattering of each little hoof, and she, too, sprinted outside. The three of us formed an impenetrable donkey wall.

Well, actually, we waved our arms and screamed like lunatics.

It was enough. Jo-Jo and Foggy took one look and decided they wanted nothing to do with these shrieking, hysterical women. They made a sharp right turn into the driveway of a shocked elderly man who won't look me in the eye to this day, no matter how many times I run past his house.

My neighbor then retrieved a couple of halters and lead ropes from her barn, and within five minutes Jo-Jo and Foggy's excellent adventure had ended.

Soon thereafter, my friendship with Sam did, too.

That was the casualty.

It wasn't working. The divorce was too fresh. I waited a few months, and then tried again, had coffee with a man I met on Craigslist. He was smart, handsome, athletic, employed. He seemed to like me. He was not averse to the idea of donkeys.

I cried all the way home.

A sure sign you're not ready to get out there: when you spend most of the evening trying to convince your date to reconcile with his ex-wife.

At the end of my marriage, I didn't want to be married. But now that I'm divorced, I don't want to be divorced.

Having lived it for a year, seen its effects on my kids, I've become a radical, wild-eyed, foaming-mouthed crusader for lifelong marriage, whether you're happy or not. I start a Facebook page for Jo-Jo and Foggy: Donkeys Against Divorce. I pen articles for the Coalition for Divorce Reform. My friends stop complaining to me about their husbands.

I'm a mess. I'm a newly divorced, emotionally bankrupt, serially broke, unemployed, single mother of four; a southern girl marooned deep in New England, a thousand miles from her family and closest friends. For reasons I can't fully explain, there are two donkeys in my backyard.

Probably.

The donkeys are hungry. So am I. I'm dieting today, at least until noon, and I'd very much like to take to my bed.

But I've registered for this half-marathon three months away, forked over eighty dollars I could have spent on Breyer's ice cream or ten bales of hay, and I suppose I'm going to have to train for it so I can whip some thirty-three-year-old butt.

Which is why I'm lying flat on the floor in my three-season room—sun on my face, dust on the floor, completely and utterly inert.

I don't want to train. I don't even want to run. I can't do it. The farthest I've run this year was five miles, and it was not a pleasant experience. This morning, I weighed 158 pounds. (But who's counting?) I've gained four pounds in two months. The numbers are going the wrong way. What was I thinking? My feet hurt. My heart hurts. I'll never be able to run thirteen miles again, let alone beat anyone under the age of eighty-three.

It is a pity party of one. My invisible coach refuses to participate.

"Get up," Pre says to me harshly. "Get up, and go change your clothes."

I roll over in a show of defiance and lie on my stomach for a while, the sun sympathetically warming my shoulders.

When Pre ran for the University of Oregon, the legend was that every time he stepped on the track, the sun would come out, even if it had been cloudy all day.

I was twelve; I wouldn't know. I only know I don't feel like running today.

But I can't lie here on the floor until the kids come home. The room is all glass, and the neighbors can see in. Worse, the coach in my head is growing increasingly surly.

"Get going," he snarls.

I sit up miserably and trudge up the stairs to my closet, my legs heavy and dull. I have barely started to prepare for the race, but already it feels like I'm training too much.

That's what happens when you're directed by a phantom coach for whom a light workout was "an easy ten."

That's ten miles. Not ten minutes.

My hero George Sheehan said his pain threshold was a firm hand-shake. Steve Prefontaine didn't seem to have one. His secret, his coach and teammates always said, was an astonishing ability to ignore pain. "Somebody may beat me, but they're going to have to bleed to do it," he said.

This is going to be bad.

The first thing my inner coach tells me is that if I'm going to run a half-marathon without embarrassing myself, I'll have to run more and run longer.

Harrumph. Sounds like a college kid with no family and no job. A rube who's got nothing else to do but run. Besides, this is elementary stuff. I could have told myself this.

But dammit, he's right.

For two years, most of my runs have been four miles in fifty or so minutes: nothing to sneeze at, maybe, but undeniably a comfortable rut. The last time I ran Kiawah, it took me two hours and seventeen minutes to cover 13.1 miles, and I was thrilled with that.

But that was five years, two children, and a divorce ago. Unless I signed up for severe pain on December 11—and, just for the record, I did not—I need to get used to sustained and varied effort again.

Pre's right. He will always be right.

Damn him.

Pre and me, we're a match made in Purgatory. Purgatory, of course, is that in-between state, neither heaven nor hell, which the Catechism of the Catholic Church says exists for the purification of a newly dead soul. It's a great concept. I need purifying; I suppose the great Steve Prefontaine does, too.

If you believe in heaven and hell and such things, it's not such a stretch to believe that Pre, who died alone at twenty-four, pinned under his overturned car, departed this world and went straight to Purgatory. The Church says Purgatory is for people who die "in God's grace and friendship, but still imperfectly purified." But it doesn't say where Purgatory is.

If I were God, and I needed to purify someone, I'm pretty sure I'd send him right back to Earth.

What better task could there be for a childless, chiseled, hard-driving Olympian than to have to train a frumpy middle-aged mother who can't do a dozen sit-ups and would expire from happiness if she ever achieved a nine-minute mile?

There is a God, and he's in a celestial armchair somewhere with a giant bowl of popcorn, slapping his holy thigh and roaring with laughter at the zany antics on Earth.

Alarmingly, it seems I'm the joke.

Remember my failed attempts to find a live, breathing coach? If Alberto Salazar had answered my letter and taken me on, or if I'd found a college coach who'd let me train with his team, this would never have happened.

I'd have done my assigned workouts, iced my injuries, cursed the day I ever thought of this dumb idea, and, at the end of the day, gone home to care for my family, free from further coach interference.

There'd be none of this twenty-four/seven stuff. No Coach Salazar or Coach Benoit Samuelson glowering over me when I lie inert on the floor.

But when I started talking to Pre, I unwittingly signed up for non-stop needling and harassment. This was a man, who, in four years at the University of Oregon, never missed a workout for a cold or illness. A man who ran every morning at six o'clock at a six-minute-mile pace, no matter what time he'd gone to bed the night before.

Of course, when Pre was up late, it was because he was out partying. I'm up late stroking the hair of a perspiring child with strep throat, and wondering what her father is doing.

My cause being nobler, I think Pre should cut me some slack. But he doesn't care about my circumstances. All Pre cares about is the run.

He wasn't always that way. In junior high school, in Coos Bay, Oregon, he famously watched the cross-country team run by and said, "What kind of crazy nut would spend two or three hours a day just running?" Tom Jordan recounts this in his biography *Pre*.

Later that year, though, Steve had to run laps in PE class, and had a change of heart when he realized he was one of the fastest kids. His destiny, it turned out, was to become one of those crazy nuts.

Four years later, Jordan writes, Steve was a senior track star and a fixture on the streets of Coos Bay. To locals, he was "the kid who never stopped running."

Besides his physical gifts, Pre has another, one not everyone has. He has the capacity to change. He will change, over time, coaching me.

He will soften, become kinder, more patient, less sardonic. But that will take months. Now he's glowering at my dinner plate, snorting contemptuously when I stir three teaspoons of sugar into my coffee.

But unpleasant as he is right now, the kid's good for something. He pushes me out the door. This is an amazing feat, not only because of my unwillingness to suffer, but because I outweigh him.

I weigh 158 today. At the time of his death, Pre weighed 154.

By comparison, Galen Rupp, Oregon's latest blond wonder kid, weighs 138. My dream weight, coincidentally.

With Rupp positioned between us, Pre and I would be chunky bookends. Thinking this, I smile to myself ruefully. Finally, something in common. A shared bond between dissimilar souls galaxies apart.

But still. Pre ran a four-minute mile, and I can barely crack ten. I know what's coming. Oh yes.

He's going to insist that I bleed.

sixteen

Don't Cross Me

In her spiritual memoir *The Bread of Angels,* Stephanie Saldaña says she always knows when her otherworld revelations are true, "because the voice is telling you the single sentence you are least prepared to hear."

I understand that. I know my coach is true, is real, because he's always telling me to do the thing I am least prepared to do.

Like cross-training.

The first task Pre assigned me was to break up my routines. Shatter my rut.

Done. No problem. Instead of the same old four miles three times a week, I'm running six miles one day, then three another, then six, then two. I'm getting in more miles, but staggering the length, so I'm not running my body down like I would if I'd just piled on more miles.

But that was last week.

This week, he wants me to spend more time on my feet. A lot more.

Surely he jests. I'm a single mother of four. Unless I'm writing, there's not a moment of the day I'm not on my feet. You can't muck stalls in a lounge chair. I'm *always* Homo erecta.

Unamused, he stares me down.

Let's just get this over with so I can get out of here.

Instructions. I'm to work out—at least once a week—for two hours or more at a time. The activity doesn't matter; in fact, it's best to do different things. Just exercise, hard, for 120 minutes or more.

No sweat. Sure thing. I can do this easily, since I'm already accustomed to exercising for an hour. What's another hour?

What's another straw on the camel?

With confidence approaching hubris, I head outside for a personal triathlon. First, I run my usual four miles and stretch a bit: calves, quads, hamstrings, obliques.

Then a change of clothes. I don a swimsuit, my daughter's long-sleeved surfing shirt, and a pair of shorts. I slip on a helmet and ride my bike two miles to the lake.

Now, I, über-mom, shall swim.

We pause briefly for a weather report.

You should know, this being New England, the lake at Hopkinton State Park is barely tolerable in July. It's now late September, winter is coming on fast, and so it's not so much a lake as a gigantic, black ice bath. No one is in the water, not even the Canada geese.

But I'm still hot and flushed from my run. It's no problem. I plunge in, and find I was wrong.

It's not a lake.

It's a lake-sized Slushee.

I thrash around miserably, trying to get warm. The only good thing about fat is its ability to insulate, but mine, indignant at the unannounced ice capades, has ordered a work stoppage and gone on strike.

I shiver. My toes are turning blue and will soon fall off and float to the surface, tasty morsels for the Canada geese. Must. Get. Out.

But my coach is glaring at me.

Pre, deprived of life long before his time, thinks it would be wonderful to be alive today, even hurting. What he wouldn't give to be fifty-nine years old today, plunging into an icy lake, shuddering in the bracing, black water.

"Get over yourself," he says darkly.

I understand. My eyes soften in sympathy. I get over myself.

I plunge deeper, splay horizontal, and begin to swim, whispering to myself, "Suck it up, suck it up."

The Slushee envelopes me. I think of Al Stewart's song "Antarctica": *The hopeless quest of Shackleton and the dream-like death of Scott.*

I'm coming to join you, Mr. Scott.

Suck it up, suck it up, suck it up.

But wait. In a few minutes, the water seems strangely warmer. A few more, and it's—dare I say?—pleasant.

Ten minutes later, I flip onto my back and float on the Slushee, the sun rushing to sooth and anoint my flushed face. No longer cold, I am at peace. I am BAAAAAAAD.

I don't stay long, no more than twenty minutes. Truth is, I'm an inefficient and ungainly swimmer, and I wear myself out pretty quickly. But I ride my bike home, triumphant. Heck, if this is all it takes, in two months I'm going to look like freakin' Madonna.

But reality always comes to call the next day, its hand stuck out for Advil. And then I remember why I don't exercise for two hours each day, and it has nothing to do with a lack of time.

Basically, it's this: Nothing kills ambition like exhaustion.

This has happened many times before: a hard workout, euphoria, dreams of grandeur, legs of clay. That's how I learned it's easier to stay in my safe rut. Four miles, three or four times a week. Same old comfortable pace. Easy on the legs, easy on the ego.

But I'll never make it through Kiawah like that.

So three days after my personal triathlon, with Pre's nudging, I decide to do it again. I pack the ibuprofen and drive to Cape Cod, where I will ride my bike for two hours on the gorgeous rail-trail.

All right: I'll grudgingly admit there's one good thing about divorce, and it may be the real reason it's so prevalent today. Three words: every other weekend. For an exhausted, stressed-out parent, is there any greater gift?

I suppose I should explain the bike. It was a gift from my friend Sam, who is one of those obsessive-compulsive cyclists who bike everywhere: to work, to the grocery store, to visit a college two states away.

When we became friends, Sam, wanting to share my experiences, signed up for horseback-riding lessons and resumed running, even though he'd badly broken his ankle years ago and wasn't supposed to run anymore.

Naturally, Sam thought that I, possessed of two fresh-from-the-factory ankles, should reciprocate and take up cycling. I had no interest. I also had no bike. Undaunted, he bought me one for Christmas.

I hadn't ridden a bike since I was ten, and the only kind I knew was Huffy. But Sam, who is OCD like that, had a Specialized bike custom-fitted for me, right down to the length of my legs. He figured I was only one good ride away from biking-nerd-dom.

Even knowing nothing about bicycles, I had to admit it was a beautiful piece of metal: silver and gray titanium, with a high-tech odometer, a padded saddle, and a little black gear bag stuffed with all sorts of gadgets I still don't know how to use. And it was amazingly light, just a few pounds; I could lift it easily with one hand.

What I couldn't do was ride the infernal thing.

It was a bicycle for serious cyclists, which meant no kickstand (who knew?) and pedals designed by de Sade. You couldn't just put on some sneakers and ride it. Oh no.

You had to put on special bike shoes, with little metal clamps that locked into clips on the pedals. The idea is, when your feet are attached like this, your calves circle more efficiently and you can go faster. Sam assured me that it was simple to learn, that I'd be zooming around in an hour.

I zoomed, all right. Damn, that pavement is hard.

I couldn't get the hang of the pedals. I'd clip in, and my heart would seize up with terror, and I'd flop over on the ground, my feet still bound to the bike. If they'd attached the guys at Guantánamo Bay to this bike, the United Nations would have been in a rage.

After a few scraped knees—believe me, there's nothing sexier than a middle-aged mother with scabby knees—the bike was relegated to the back of the barn, behind the lawn mower and leaf blower, to escape only on occasion.

Besides my own ineptitude with clip-on pedals, there's also the problem of Scary Bike News. You know. Scary Bike News is all over the place, every single week.

Example. Some outstanding citizen, a father of eight who picks up trash on the side of the road every Saturday and volunteers at the local senior center, is riding his bike to work to reduce his carbon imprint, and wham, he's mowed down by a newly licensed teenager.

I don't *look* for these stories; they leap out at me and shake my shoulders, shrieking, "Are you *sure* you really want to ride that bike?"

It's not so much that I'm scared of dying. I'm equally distressed at the prospect of breaking my leg. Which is why, even though everyone says you should cross-train, even though Pre has *ordered* me to cross-train, I've always been reluctant to do anything but run.

The idea behind cross-training is simple: To excel at one sport, you should participate in many. That way, you work your heart and lungs continually without overstressing your joints. Sign me up, right? Makes sense, and sounds vaguely like fun.

Furthermore, I have no excuses. I am well-equipped to cross-train. I have the bike. I have Rollerblades. I have ice skates. I have a jump rope. I have a floor on which to do sit-ups. I have two lakes to swim in within a mile of my house.

And of course, I have donkeys—and sometimes, a horse— requiring hours of grooming and manure shoveling, a fantastic upper-body workout that surpasses every Cybex machine at the Y.

But for me, these things aren't so much tools for cross-training as my personal kick-the-bucket list. For someone as naturally unathletic as me, the instruments of cross-training are actually quite dangerous.

Take the horse.

The horse, by the way, is why we have donkeys. If you've been wondering, that's the answer. Got donkeys? Blame a horse.

We got Jo-Jo to keep the horse company. Then we got Foggy to keep Jo-Jo company. Then the horse left. So today, even though what

I *really* want is one horse, what I have is two donkeys.

Somewhere in there, there's a metaphor for my life.

Anyway, we went through two horses, trying to find one. The first, Dunkin, was an enormous gray draft horse, fresh off an Amish farm. He lasted a month.

It turned out, although he'd pulled wagons in Pennsylvania for ten years, Dunkin had been under saddle (that is, broken to ride) for less than six months. I learned this after my first ride, when Dunkin decided, without notifying me, that it was time to go home, and he took off galloping down the center of the road, with me shrieking and clinging to his neck for dear life.

Dunkin, bless his heart, had a nice new home the next week. I hope his new owners are still alive.

Dante lasted longer. He came from a lesson barn in western Massachusetts. Since children had ridden him without incident, he, of course, would make a great family horse, calm and safe. His classified ad called him the "Deal of the Year!" His owner told me, with a straight face, that she had too many horses and needed some quick cash so her son could go to Europe on a school trip.

Oh, the stories you'll believe when you're looking for a bombproof horse.

If I've learned anything over the past five years, it's this: There's no such thing as a bombproof marriage. And there's no such thing as a bombproof horse.

Dante, the Deal of the Year, lived in the backyard with Jo-Jo for nearly two years, happy to devour my hay and destroy my fences when he wasn't busy trying to kill me. He was a mean old buzzard. He kicked my daughter the first week and kicked the farrier a month later. But it was me he really wanted to snuff out.

We'd set off for a ride on the magnificent equestrian trails that begin, literally, across the street from my house, and ten yards down the path he'd stop cold. Then, ignoring my crop, my kicks, and my increasingly desperate commands, he'd pivot off the trail and back into the woods, aiming for the nearest tree. He was trying to brush me off.

I was the fly; he was the swatter.

At first, Michael didn't believe me when I announced the Deal of the Year was trying to kill me. He thought I was exaggerating, over-reacting. So one day, I insisted he follow us across the street and watch. "Yup," Michael agreed after a few minutes. "He's trying to kill you."

Two years of seventy-dollar-an-hour horse training later, I finally gave up and gave Dante away. I hope his new owner is still alive.

Bad as he was, Dante's leaving was another blow. More failure, more loss. I was disappointed, not only because I've been crazy about horses since I was a child, but because equestrians are famously skinny. (When's the last time you saw a fat jockey?) I'd hoped regular riding would cross-train me, condition my inner thighs, and tighten my glutes.

But given my emotional state at the time, to continue to ride Dante, the Deal of the Year, was to attempt suicide by horse. Like the last year of my marriage, Dante left bruises. There's nothing quite so dangerous as a bad horse.

Not that running can't also maim you. I've gotten bruises from running, too.

Once, I was running in unfamiliar territory in Columbia, on a poorly maintained sidewalk with dusk coming on. Going too fast down a hill, my foot caught in a wide crack, and I tripped, landing facedown on concrete.

I got up, limping, dizzy and bleeding, and realized I couldn't make it the two miles back home, so I staggered up the driveway of the closest home and knocked on the door. A woman peered out the glass at my bloody face, probably wondering if she'd forgotten Halloween.

But as luck would have it, I fell in front of the home of a registered nurse. She opened the door, called her husband to bring towels and ice. Then they called Michael, who came quickly, took me home, administered ibuprofen, and put me to bed.

The next day, we visited a plastic surgeon who said my swollen nose would be better in a week. The black eyes and the bruises lasted a little longer.

I had a job interview two weeks later, and I went in looking like I'd gone the distance with Apollo Creed.

But I learned many new things from the experience. First, you should always have some form of identification on you when you run, even if it's just a phone number scratched in ink on your running shoes.

Second, ignore platitudes. If you're a runner, pride comes *after* a fall.

For a month, everywhere I went, people wanted to know what had happened to me. And, for once, I was happy to tell them.

How did I get this black eye, these purple bruises? Aw, shucks. I got these injuries—wait for it—while I was out *running*.

Oooooooh. Ahhhhhhhh. There'd be a murmur of admiration, the

noise the aliens make when they see the claw in *Toy Story.*

Or it's possible I imagined that.

But still. This was so much better than having to say that I fell down the stairs, or walked into a wall, or that my horse was trying to kill me.

Surely there is nothing nobler than to suffer for one's sport. Up until this point, I'd never had the privilege.

When I was twenty-four, I fell off a horse and had to have stitches. But that was nothing compared with this. I love riding, but, like golf and NASCAR, it only masquerades as a sport. It's not. It doesn't get your heart up and running for a sustained amount of time. It's not an aerobic activity.

Running, however, is, and it requires coordination and stamina. To go for a run and come back looking like you were hit by a truck— hey, that takes a real athlete.

A real athlete, say, like me.

Truth is, I'd always been vaguely envious of people who run while injured. You know the ones: They hobble up the street with determined, pinched faces, with wrapped ankles and bandaged knees.

Alas, that had never been me.

Despite the wide load my legs carry, I've never had a shin splint or plantar fasciitis. I did have bursitis once; of course, a point of pride. For a while, I got to work the phrase *my orthopedic surgeon* into every conversation.

But bursitis was invisible. It required only painkillers and steroid shots, not bandages. If I want conspicuous injuries, it seems I'll have to increase my mileage.

Like you should be out doing right now, Pre crossly interjects.

I scowl.

I ache. Invisibly, of course.

After my personal triathlon, and then the long bike ride on Cape Cod, I'd given myself too many days off. Ironic, I know.

The experts say our bodies need twenty-four to forty-eight hours after a hard workout to recover, to rebuild.

After three days of immobility, however, inertia sets in. The joints stiffen. The muscles contract. Resurrect, Nature says, or your body will begin to rot in the tomb.

So far, the laws of physics have done nothing to help me lose weight. But one of them is unerringly true: A body in motion remains in motion; a body at rest remains at rest.

Three centuries ago, Sir Isaac Newton told us that for the motion of an object (say, *me*) to change, a force (say, *the fear of weighing four hundred pounds*) must act upon it. He also conveyed the exceedingly bad news that the acceleration produced by that force is inversely proportional to the mass of the body.

Translation: If I want to run Kiawah, and run it well, I need to inverse my mass. Lose some weight.

A light goes on in my head, and it's florescent and a thousand watts.

In the beginning, I ran to try to lose weight. Now it's reversed: I need to lose weight so I can run. At least so I can run longer and faster than I do.

There it is again: the thing I least want to hear.

You know what this means: Diet tomorrow.

Ice cream tonight.

seventeen

Bad Magic Food

You thin people will never understand this, but it's the truth: There has never dawned a Monday on which I wasn't on a diet.

At least until 11 AM.

Oh, there have been a few exceptions. I didn't actively diet while I was pregnant, or when strapped to a bed in the ICU. But otherwise, I begin each week on a diet.

Now, it's true that some weeks, I diet more vigorously than others. On occasion, I go to the trouble of stocking the refrigerator with radishes and celery and hummus and other unappetizing things. More often, though, I don't prepare, just harbor a vague resolution to eat less and exercise more.

What I'm doing, really, is hoping. Hoping that people are wrong when they say the best predictor of future outcomes is past behavior. Hoping that people can indeed change, grow, mature, turn on a dime. Hoping there is light after the bitter divorce, after the car flips on top of you, after you've eaten three fully iced gingerbread men.

Dum spiro spero, the motto of South Carolina. Attributed to Cicero, it's Latin for "While I breathe, I hope."

And, as a native South Carolinian, I hope. Earnestly, devoutly, steadfastly. Ignoring a growing suspicion that hope, despite its press, is actually a wicked, monstrous thing.

This is the week, I'm hoping. The momentous, life-changing week in which I will push past all obstacles and break through to the glorious, thin new me that's waiting to emerge on Friday.

Of course, in our family, Friday is Pizza Night, which might be part of the problem.

Given that there's no Salad Night.

Talking about failed diets is embarrassing, because the physics of dieting—eat less, exercise more!—are so basic, so simple, that any second-grader should be able to master them.

Equation. If it is the case (*and it is*) that I want to be thin so that I can run better, and if it is the case (*and it is*) that I will lose weight if I drastically cut back my portions, where's the problem? What's so difficult about that?

Why can't I bring myself to make the necessary changes—even better, the *temporary* necessary changes—that will bring my goals within reach?

If you can answer that question correctly, please let me know, so we can do an infomercial together and become fabulously rich.

Because it's not just me starting a diet every Monday; it's two-thirds of the country. An estimated 65 to 70 percent of adult Americans are either obese or overweight, despite the fevered pleadings of our doctors.

But thank God for fat people. If we were all to wake up skinny tomorrow, where would all the Zumba instructors work? In America, we spend fifty-eight billion dollars each year on weight loss products and services. Why? No one but Mike Huckabee has gotten any skinnier.

Our national girth, our collective inability to lose weight, is a seemingly unsolvable riddle. An oxymoron: It's not about the food. But it is.

Few of us eat too much because we're hungry. We eat because we're lonely, sad, happy, nervous, relieved, tense, tired, bored, procrastinating.

When asked to vacuum or take out the trash, my previously satiated children suddenly find themselves starving, unable to drag their emaciated selves off the couch without first having a snack.

Children themselves can make parents fat. Not just from pregnancy, but from their continued existence. Pesky little things, they insist on eating—sometimes, several times a day.

Worse, they tell other people what they are eating. Their teachers, their friends, their doctor.

Our doctor—I call her Glamour, MD—is a size 0–2 *after* the holidays, and always wears mascara, high heels, and short skirts. In my next life, I want to be her.

But when I take the children in for their annual checkups, not only does she insist on *weighing* them, but then, during the examination, she asks what kinds of foods they eat.

She asks *them,* mind you, not me.

If she were to ask me, I would say, "Greek yogurt, brown rice, steamed kale, and wild Alaskan salmon. Every meal. What can I say? They're creatures of habit."

But no. She asks them. The truth will out, and sometimes it involves white bread.

Today, I have eaten one bowl of Honey Nut Cheerios, two pieces of Pepperidge Farm Carb-Style bread (with Olivio and jam), three tablespoons of chicken salad, an unknown number of Wheat Thins, a handful of salted almonds, and a frosted gingerbread man. It's nothing Oprah's chef would prepare, but not an insane amount of food, don't you agree? And, of course, I am occasionally mobile.

The problem is, I eat all that, and *then* also what I prepare for the kids. This morning, we had French toast, scrambled eggs, and berries. Tonight, we'll have spaghetti.

In my twenties, when I first started running and lost weight, I was single and working in an office, so I ate lunch at a restaurant every weekday. At night, I'd have cereal and fruit. I never felt deprived. My satisfying lunches kept cravings at bay.

Also, it helped that there was no Cap'n Crunch in the house.

But soon after I started marching in the right dietary direction, I got married and started a family, and everything changed. For the worse. I was either eating for two, or preparing for five, and my nurturing instincts took over.

Maybe you're like me? My nurturing template, inherited from my mother and grandmother, is food.

It's easy to see how the template is made. Families fly apart for work and school; they come together when it's time to eat. Our most important relationships are built around food.

In my family, there are three staples of conversation: the weather, what we're eating now, and what we'll be eating next. I come by it honestly, at least.

Even my chosen worship of God revolves around wine and bread. "On all social levels sharing a table is the first sign of membership in a group," writes Italian professor Massimo Montanari in *Food Is Culture*.

Food matters.

I came to marriage believing what my grandmother taught by example: that a good southern wife should prepare hot and fattening meals. And so I did, and still do. I cook dinner most nights, brunch on Sunday, and a hot breakfast on weekdays. Friday is Pancake Day.

Yeah, yeah, I know. Everyone can see the problem but me.

There is no Granola Day.

But in my defense, and the defense of mothers everywhere, dieting is particularly hard on our kind. Rare is the woman who has both young children and a pantry free of Kraft mac-and-cheese. And you can only say no to Oreos in the grocery store so many times before you feel like an ogre.

You buy them for the kids, yes. But then they're at school, and then at soccer and piano, and you're at home, and you walk by the Oreos, and they look so lonely and dejected, and soon—out of nothing more than pity—you're hiding in the pantry, comforting the Oreos and their forlorn creamy centers. Comforting yourself.

Ants, I tell the kids. Ants got into the Oreos again. Gotta get a new exterminator.

Oreos, mac-and-cheese, and Ore-Ida Tater Tots are Bad Magic Food, like the Turkish Delight that Edmund gobbles when he visits Narnia in C. S. Lewis's classic *The Lion, the Witch and the Wardrobe.* As Edmund learns, with tragic results, "There's nothing that spoils the taste of good ordinary food half as much as the memory of bad magic food."

Of course, good ordinary food can be magical, too. I love raspberries, blueberries, spinach, almonds, tomatoes, well-prepared chicken, and brown rice studded with walnuts.

But not if I've just eaten the sugary, creamy flan my oldest daughter makes.

It is my own Turkish Delight. A cup of it, and I renounce all fruits and vegetables.

Bad Magic Food does that to you. Once you taste it, you lose your desire for Good Ordinary Food. To my knowledge, C. S. Lewis never had a significant weight problem, but he had a keen understanding of people who do.

Beyond that, there's the cost. Bad Magic Food is cheap. Good Ordinary Food can be expensive. Compare the price of ramen noodles for five with that of wild Alaskan salmon for five, and you understand why the poorest of us tend to be the fattest.

So, Pre? Really, just shut up.

It was fine for you to grow your own salad greens outside your humble trailer. *You weren't feeding four kids,* two of whom don't like salad.

Besides, you're a mesomorph. I'm an endomorph. And after reading about body types, I'm beginning to wonder if it's not my weight that's the problem, but my God-given shape.

My God-*inflicted* shape.

Twenty-four hundred years ago, Hippocrates sorted humans by shape, but it was the twentieth-century American psychologist W. H. Sheldon who made somatotyping his whole career. Sheldon is the evil genius who labeled us mesomorphs, endomorphs, and ectomorphs.

If you read Sheldon—I *don't* recommend it—do not get his *Atlas of Men,* which contains a thousand photographs of largely unattractive naked men and is the closest thing available to pornography at your public library.

I checked it out, and my librarians are still giving me strange looks.

Instead, get Sheldon's *The Varieties of Temperament,* which has more words, fewer ugly naked men. Reading *Varieties,* I learned that between Dr. Sheehan, Pre, and me, we've got all the somatotypes covered.

Dr. Sheehan was an ectomorph, characterized by "fragility, linearity, flatness of chest and delicacy throughout the body."

Translation: I couldn't have married him. If I'd rolled over on him during the night, I'd have killed him.

Pre was a mesomorph, compact and muscular. Translation: an incredible hunk.

I, endomorph, am round and fat. Consequently, I "float high in water."

Thanks, Dr. Sheldon. Thanks a lot.

It's hard not to feel slighted. Given a choice (which I wasn't), I'd rather have delicate limbs than the dubious talent of easily remaining afloat.

But hey, if I'm ever shipwrecked, I'm covered.

More troubling, Sheldon—like my lifelong nemesis, my evil-eyed scale—seems to think I can never be skinny. Diets, schmiets, he says, in a little more scholarly manner.

"Endomorphs are usually fat, but they are sometimes seen emaciated," he writes. "In the latter event, they do not change into mesomorphs or ectomorphs any more than a starved mastiff will turn into a spaniel or collie."

I don't want to be a collie. I just want to be thin.

But hell, he's probably right. I see the truth when I stand in front of a full-length mirror. There, when I run my hands down the contour of my hips and smash all the fat to middle, my fundamental shape is still wavy, not straight.

Of course, "wavy" is an understatement. "Tsunami-y" is more like it.

But I understand what Sheldon is saying. There is such a thing as big-boned; it's not just a euphemism for *fat*. There are indeed hips designed especially for birthin' babies. These would be mine. They're why, if God had not stopped me via hysterectomy, I'd probably have 12 kids, like Mrs. Sheehan.

Once upon a time, in cultures far, far away, hips like mine were valued. Now no one values them, not even me. Peter Paul Rubens is long dead.

I feel sad, for a moment, for my unloved and unappreciated hips. They've done so much for me. In the past. Now, dammit, they're slowing me down.

I think of my petite friend Laura, the pants lady, who has run a zillion Boston Marathons. She looks like a runner. Her hips are linear and compact.

I try to picture her with fifty more pounds. Where would they go?

I Photoshop Laura in my mind. Puff out her cheeks. Widen her thighs. Poof out her abdomen. But despite my Photoshop fattening, her hips are still straight, not tsunami-y. She, a lithe collie, can't become a mastiff.

It's hopeless, my shape. It's not Bad Magic Food. It's genetics. It has absolutely nothing to do with what I'm eating.

Walking away, Pre smirks.

eighteen

Pre Lives

Walk into any running-supply store, and chances are somewhere on the wall is a poster of Steve Roland Prefontaine. He will be in motion, blond hair rippling in the wind.

Although Pre died in 1975, every high school distance runner knows the name, and the story of how he died, even if they can't quite articulate why he's still loved today.

Prefontaine was, many believe, America's greatest distance runner. When he smashed his sports car into a rock on May 30, 1975, he held fourteen track-and-field records, and no American had beaten him at a distance more than a mile in five years.

He was a gutsy, gritty runner, with uneven legs, who had not come naturally to the sport. At Marshfield High School in Coos Bay, Oregon, he ran cross-country as a freshman and came in an undistinguished fifty-third in the state meet.

But by the next year, biographer Tom Jordan said, Pre was "thoroughly hooked on running" (rats like us), and by his junior year he went undefeated and became, and remained, a star until his tragic end.

Like Princess Diana and President John F. Kennedy, a startling death ensured his legend.

Had Pre lived, he'd be a member of the AARP now, asking for the seniors' discount at Denny's. He'd be bald, or close to it. He might limp. Even well preserved, infused with the magical elixir of the well exercised, the glorious specimen of youth that was Pre would be considerably diminished.

Would I dream about a sixty-year-old Steve Prefontaine at night? I'm so sorry. But probably not.

Ironically, if Pre were alive today, I might not even know anything about him.

He was supposed to run to glory at the 1976 Olympics, after underperforming in Munich in '72. But who knows?

Muscles tear. Arches fall. (Marriages dissolve.) Heroes fail. He could have finished third again, or not even placed. He could have slipped into obscurity, just another of Bill Bowerman's "hamburgers."

But he didn't. He died as flamboyantly as he ran, and his persona is forevermore etched on a rock.

In 1975, the number one song was "Love Will Keep Us Together" by the Captain and Tennille. Gerald Ford was president. *Sanford and Son* was still on TV.

It's been thirty-seven years.

Ask any high school sprinter who the Captain and Tennille are, and chances are they won't know. But how they love Steve Prefontaine.

At the University of Oregon gift shop, right now, today, you can buy shirts that say STOP PRE, GO PRE, PRE LIVES and PRE LIVES IN ME.

On the Internet, you can buy a PRE LIVES? shirt with a crude sketch of an overturned car. I see it and wince.

Not being a high school track-and-field athlete, I didn't grow up steeped in Pre lore. I doubt my mother and grandmother knew who he was, even back then. I was ten in 1972, and we watched the Olympics that year, but my family followed swimming, not distance running. Our hero was a guy named Mark Spitz.

Spitz won seven gold metals in Munich, then retired at age twenty-two. He's still alive, at least as I'm writing. But so far as I know, you can't buy a T-shirt that says SPITZ LIVES. Life's funny like that.

Even when I started running, it would be years before I encountered Steve Prefontaine. I was busy reading Dr. Sheehan, who quoted Emerson and Ortega and William James, not the rube from Coos Bays.

But I do subscribe to running magazines, and they all still regularly pay homage to Pre. Being a hot-blooded American woman, albeit one pushing menopause, it wasn't long before his picture, then his story, caught my attention.

The guy, let's admit it, was hot. I could have done without the sideburns, but the blond hair and the biceps were the stuff of middle-aged women's fantasies, and that's even before you don the speed goggles.

More than hot, he was *interesting*. I didn't care much about his fight with the Amateur Athletic Union over pay for amateur athletes. That was too esoteric and beyond my range of interest.

I didn't even care about his records.

But I loved that this world-class, world-famous athlete grew his own salad greens and drove old, beat-up cars. That he lived, unembarrassed, in a trailer. That he built a sauna in his garage, took his dog to class. That, despite his growing fame, he kept his ego in check and worked hard at menial, blue-collar jobs.

And when I learned he'd secretly, quietly, been training inmates at a local prison, that was it: Swoosh, like the Nike emblem. Swoosh, there went my heart.

Like an adolescent cross-country runner, I fell in love with my coach.

The T-shirt clinched it.

When Pre-mania was at its peak, his fans wore T-shirts that said GO PRE. As a joke, some people had shirts made that said STOP PRE and wore them to the Olympic Trials at Hayward Field in Eugene.

Some fans were offended, but not Prefontaine. After winning the race, he trotted over to a man who was waving a STOP PRE shirt, took it from him, and put it on. He ran his victory laps in it.

How do you *not* love a guy like that?

But I love him with eyes wide open, with the reservations of maturity.

The guy could run, sure, but he was just a kid, and, if you've read any of his writing, you know he was no scholar. The Prefontaine quote so often printed on T-shirts and posters—"To give anything less than your best is to sacrifice the gift"—quite frankly, puts me to sleep. The guy needed a writer.

And I can never forget that Pre's blood-alcohol level at the time of his fatal crash was said to be over the Oregon limit. His family and supporters disputed the coroner's ruling, but no one denied he'd been drinking beer in the hours leading up to the crash.

Steve Prefontaine, my hero and coach, may have, in fact, been killed by a drunk driver—himself.

There are theories of another car, another driver, forcing him off the road, flipping him into the rock. Others speculate he could have just been changing the radio station. But remember, whatever the cause, in a one-car accident, the driver is ultimately at fault.

You probably know all the rest.

How a neighbor heard a car crash and ran to assist. How he couldn't lift the car off Pre's chest, so he left to get help. How he didn't know who was under the car.

Before help arrived, the greatest long-distance runner in America had died alone, pinned under his MGB. It was, perhaps, the most horrific way imaginable for this young man to die: those remarkable lungs crushed, that extraordinary strength rendered useless. A senseless sacrifice of his own tremendous gift.

When Dr. Sheehan introduced me to Pre on that West Virginia hill, I knew only a little bit about him. I had a vague image of what he looked like, what he represented, what he'd done, what had happened. But my curiosity was piqued.

Over the next few months, I read a few books about him and rented two films about his life: *Without Limits* and *Fire on the Track*. I watched clips of him on the Internet, video of him running, interviews he gave. On a family trip to the West Coast, I even visited Eugene, Oregon, and visited the places where he lived and died.

For someone with such fire in his belly, Pre, like Dr. Sheehan, seemed surprisingly shy, even gentle at times.

That may or may not have been the real Pre, but it was the Pre I cultivated in my mind.

It was the Pre I needed.

For so long, my life at home had been hell. It was like living in a house studded with grenades. I tiptoed around in perpetual dread, awaiting the next explosion.

The people who could have hugged me, smoothed my hair, whispered I was going to be all right, all lived a thousand miles away. I had to find kindness in my own head. I had to find it in Pre.

On YouTube, I watched an interview he gave in 1973 after winning the LA Times Classic. He had to be tired and eager to leave, but Pre was patient and calm, answering predictable, dull questions as if they were the most important words he'd ever heard. He was self-effacing, funny, kind.

Of course, Pre's competitors never saw him that way. In the YouTube comments below that video, one observer wrote that he would have hated to run against Pre: "Constant pressure and pain."

Tell me about it, dude.

And, of course, at first, he'd been that way with me. Curt, surly, distracted. He let it be known he was not happy to be here with me.

But who would be, really? Anyone whose brilliant career and promising life was cut short, especially because of something dumb that he did, would most certainly have an attitude for the first couple of hundred years. I understood. This guy was enraged.

Enraged that he'd died so young, in such a dumb, avoidable way.

Enraged that help did not arrive in the first crucial moments while his life force was draining away.

Enraged that, instead of lolling around on a cloud, playing a harp, he was having to coach the most loathsome of creatures, an overweight, stay-at-home mother who spent most of her waking hours doing laundry and mopping floors.

Talk about sacrificing your gifts.

Early on, I was on the defensive. Pre's short life involved running and training, beer and pretty girls and fun cars. He couldn't understand the constraints laundry for six puts on one's goals and aspirations.

Nor could he comprehend the noise and chaos of a large family—
he who had one sister and didn't live long enough to have his own kids.

He could not apprehend a middle-aged woman's lifelong struggle
with weight. Or a mother's turmoil over whether to meet the needs
of her family, or those of her own.

Of course not. He was a jackrabbit. How could he know?

Jackrabbits. The original Shirtless Wonders.

They are characters in the children's book *The Country Bunny and
the Little Gold Shoes* by DuBose Heyward and Marjorie Flack. When
I was a child, it was one of my favorite books. My mother used to
read it to me every Easter.

First published in 1939, *The Country Bunny* is, ostensibly, an
Easter book, a tale about gaily colored eggs and magical rabbits who
deliver baskets all over the world. I love the watercolor pictures of
the Palace of Easter Eggs, its golden halls shimmering with hills of
pink, blue, purple, and yellow eggs.

The hero, the Country Bunny, is a little brown cottontail. All her
life, she's dreamed of becoming one of five Easter bunnies who deliver eggs all over the world.

But other rabbits—the haughty society hares and the long-legged
Jacks—laugh at her. They tell her to leave the business of delivering
eggs to the importantly tall and fast-running Jacks.

Then one day, Cottontail wakes up with twenty-one babies, with
no father figure around. To the world, it appears her dream is over.

*Then the big white rabbits and the Jacks with long legs
laughed and laughed, and they said, "What did we tell you? Only
a country rabbit would go and have all those babies. Now take*

care of them and leave Easter eggs to great big men bunnies like us." And they went away liking themselves very much.

When I was a girl, the feminist bent of the book was lost on me. Now, of course, it's subtle as a freight train.

But there's something else I didn't notice until recently. As much as it's about Easter, this is a book about *running*.

Cottontail hops to the Palace of Easter Eggs, where the wise and kind Grandfather Rabbit will choose the new Easter Bunny. His eye falls on Cottontail and her well-turned-out family, and he says, "It's too bad you have had no time to run and grow swift."

The little brown rabbit laughs. Then she whispers to her children to run away, so she can race after them and bring them back swiftly.

Spoiler alert: Cottontail becomes the fifth Easter Bunny.

Later in the book, the brave mother bunny makes an impossible journey and tumbles down a steep hill. Then the wise and kind Grandfather Rabbit presents her with a magic pair of running shoes, which enable her to perform all sorts of athletic feats.

So it's a feminist story, sure; an Easter tale, yes; but to me, it's a poignant story about this wonderful sport. About running when you don't look like the long-legged Jacks, and when people laugh at you, and when you have too many chores at home and have had no time to run and grow swift.

When I read this story to my children each Easter, just like my mother read it to me, I'm bawling before Cottontail even tumbles down the mountain, because, as a fat runner, that's just how I feel.

I can't run as fast as the long-legged Jacks, I know. But dammit, I've got as much guts as they do. Possibly, just possibly, even more.

Really, how much courage does it take for a skinny person to put on shorts or tights and run down the street?

And as for endurance, sure, the jackrabbits are faster. But in a race, I'm on my feet twice as long as they are. Shouldn't that count for something? Should someone admire *me*?

It takes a while, but the Pre in my head begins to.

I have to earn it, but as weeks pass, then months, I sense a change. He watches silently as I slog through my prescribed workouts. He observes the accumulating miles, the thickening calluses. Effort, equal to his, devoid of reward. No fans, no records, no glory. No promise of any to come. Just running. Always running. Running for the sake of the run.

There comes at last a grudging acknowledgment, an unspoken concession, that there's more to this sport than his own experience. That there's more than we see, always more. Another dimension, if you will.

One day, while reading a running magazine, I come across another Pre quote: "A lot of people run a race to see who is the fastest. I run to see who has the most guts."

There it is, in his own blunt words, the reason we'd forged this implausible union.

If it's guts you're looking for, you don't have to watch the Olympics or visit Hayward Field. Just go outside and find yourself a fat runner.

nineteen

The Problem of Pain

More miles, staggered. Cross-training. At least once a week, two hours on my feet. I have done all this, with no ill effect. Of course, with no significant positive effects, either.

My weight is unchanged, despite increasing effort, because I come from the line of Pooh. You know the Pooh song, don't you?

> *When I up, down, touch the ground, it puts me in the mood.*
> *Up, down, touch the ground, in the mood for food.*
> *I am stout, round, and I have found, speaking poundage-wise.*
> *I improve my appetite when I exercise!*

I sing this lustfully as I dress.

My coach is not amused. Next, he announces, we will increase the length and speed of my base runs.

Seems easy enough. (*While I up down, touch the ground, I'll think of things to chew!*)

The experts all say you shouldn't increase the length of your runs by more than 10 percent in any given week, and I suppose that's good advice coming from mortals. My coach, however, says I should run however long I damn well feel like it.

Pre used to tell his teammates he was going out for an "easy ten." Seems like the kind of guy to whom I should listen. The ability to do an easy 10 would sure make 13.1 seem a lot shorter. Although my weight is stable, my legs do seem slightly stronger this week.

But as my physical self improves, my emotional self is deteriorating. The date of Michael's wedding is approaching. I still haven't met the bride-to-be, although I've spent an inordinate amount of time thinking about things I'd hiss at her if I did. Then I feel ashamed and mean. I tell myself over and over: My pain is not her fault. I'm sure she's lovely and kind. I bear no ill feelings toward her.

Those are all saved for Michael.

I spend way too much time ruminating over my marriage, what went wrong, who was to blame. Always, who was to blame. I cry often, sometimes around the children.

In September, two months before the wedding, I go to Glamour, MD, for my annual physical. Shockingly, she thinks I could lose some weight. Improve my cholesterol levels. But my blood pressure and resting pulse rate are great.

Glamour, MD, knows all about my life. Hell, all of Boston does. It's on the radio five days a week. Michael has been gloating about his girlfriend all year. I turned on the radio one day to hear him say that you can judge a woman's looks by how many heads turn when she walks in the room, and that he's "dating a four-header."

I stopped listening to his station that day.

Glamour Doc asks, sympathetically, how I'm doing.

"Just fine," I say, and start to cry.

She writes me yet another prescription for an antidepressant. In the past, I didn't take them long enough to see a difference. This week, however, I had to give regrets for something Katherine couldn't do, for a reason I still can't comprehend.

I'm sorry Katherine can't be there, because she is going to be at her father's wedding.

I say the words, but they don't make sense. It's like saying, *I'm sorry Katherine can't be there, because her purple goat is slicing plaid oatmeal on the rhododendron.*

I'm sorry Katherine can't be there because her father is getting married to someone else although he is still married to me.

At least, in my heart, that's how it still feels.

I took the damn pills.

But just for a week. Again, I gave up. Miserably groggy and inert, I stuffed the bottle in a drawer filled with off-season clothes.

I know, I know. SSRIs take weeks to work, months to reach their full effect. But when you're a single mother of four training for a half-marathon, you don't have months. You don't have weeks. Single parents don't get the luxury of inertia. (Rarely do they get luxuries at all.)

I am sorry, Glamour, MD. I like and respect you, but I am making a decision that contradicts yours. I would rather be energetic and hurting, than dully placid and painlessly inert.

I've long been suspicious of happy pills and their prevalence in suburbia. One in ten Americans take antidepressants; they're the third most-written prescription today. They're the emblem of a nation that takes the pursuit of happiness way too seriously.

Some people, of course, have genuine deficiencies in the workings of their brains, and I don't begrudge these people their Lexapro. If you're mentally ill, by all means, correct it.

But for people who are neurologically typical, just not happy with their lives, SSRIs seem like a harmful, even dangerous, Band-Aid.

Pain has a purpose: to let you know when something's wrong. Taking pills to feel shiny and cheery seems like papering over a hole. The hole's still there; you just can't see it. And someday, you're going to trip and fall through it again.

I am determined to find a way through my pain without pills.

Yes, I saw a therapist. We tried to talk the pain away for nearly two years. Once, I asked for a diagnosis; she said I had "situational depression," which makes sense to me. There are real and concrete reasons for my misery. It's not that my brain chemistry is mysteriously out of whack.

But, some might argue, I take Advil for muscle pain, so what's wrong with taking pills to ease the pain of a broken heart?

Well, yes, that makes sense. And I am determined not to exude despair in front of the children.

So I tried Prozac. I was groggy.

Cymbalta. Completely inert.

Wellbutrin. Ding, ding, ding, we have a winner!

Wellbutrin didn't make me sleepy. It made me energetic. Focused. And—huzzah!—it took away my appetite.

I lost five pounds and decided I would take the stuff forever, even if my situational depression were to stand up and leave, and I had to buy the stuff on the black market.

But after two months, I stopped again. I couldn't do it. Because for me, being on antidepressants is like running on an unfamiliar road. How am I doing? How am I really doing? I can guess, but I don't really know.

Without happy pills, when I have a good day, I know *I* had a good day. On pills, I never know if I'm making progress, or it's just the pill talking. And how I'm really doing seems important. Like my resting pulse rate, it's information I need.

I'm going to have to find another way to heal my heart. Maybe what I read in the newspaper this morning will help. The headline is, "The Cure for Sadness: Pain."

"For most people, pain is not fun," the article says. "However, a recent study finds that, when you're not having fun, pain can help."

It goes on to explain a study in which several hundred people were tested to see how much pain they could tolerate from pressure or heat on their hands.

After the torture, the researchers questioned participants on their levels of happiness. It turned out, physical pain helped dull emotional pain. Kind of like the man who smashes his thumb with a hammer and then drops a boulder on his foot to make the thumb feel better.

That is great news to me, and so I suit up for a seven-mile run. If Norman Vincent Peale can't help me (and yes, I'm reading the book, I'm trying everything), maybe a hard workout can. I set off on a new route, determined to replace my emotional pain with physical ones. Yes, this smacks of masochism, but I do have a half-marathon coming up.

I cover 6.75 miles, at a 10:40 pace, without stopping or slowing at all. I feel strong and powerful and self-actualized and serene. Hey, *this* pain prescription is working!

Then later that night, when I get a terse email from Michael asking about the weekend schedule, my eyes flood with tears again.

I can't understand how *he* can stand it, the cold, business-like exchange of information between people once so affectionately and messily entwined; how he can willingly continue this life in which our children are handed off to each other like packages. Any parent's departure from a family leaves a hole, but ours, in particular, seems an unfillable chasm.

The house is too quiet, even when it's noisy. Without Michael's high-decibel energy powering the house as it had for seventeen years, it feels like our electricity has been cut, disconnected forever. We all talk louder than necessary at dinner. My oldest son sits in his dad's chair. We fill Michael's empty closet with Christmas decorations and gift wrap. We try to call it "the Christmas closet," but years later, we all still call it "Dad's closet." We only wrapping-papered the hole.

The children miss him; they are fevered with longing. When Michael calls, they race to the phone, frantic to be the one who gets the most minutes with Dad. When he picks them up for the weekend, Katherine cries for me; when he brings them home, she cries for Michael. She tapes a picture of the six of us over her bed, our last family photo together. Several room reorganizations later, it still hangs there.

In her memoir *I Remember Nothing*, Nora Ephron nails it: "The newfangled rigmarole of joint custody doesn't do anything to ease the cold reality: in order to see one parent, the divorced child must walk out on the other."

Since I rarely saw my dad when I was a child, didn't suffer the constant to-and-fro, I hadn't known. Since Michael was no longer living with us, he couldn't see.

It was a hell of a horrible thing we'd done to our kids.

And I, for one, didn't want to do it anymore. I'd seen a sign that said, NO MATTER HOW FAR YOU'VE GONE DOWN THE WRONG ROAD, TURN BACK.

A month before our divorce hearing, I threw my ego aside and suggested we pull back the papers and try one more time. No more therapy. Something that might actually work. Something drastic.

Boston had been good to us, and I loved the house, but I loved our family more. I fantasized about selling the house, rehoming the donkeys, and moving somewhere far from these memories. Somewhere our kids didn't have to pack a suitcase every other weekend.

Michael said no. The day his note arrived in the mail, I had to put a sick cat to sleep, and so I didn't cry when I opened it. I'd already used up that day's gallon of tears.

Also, there was this, a curious sentence: "Like marriage, divorce isn't always permanent," he wrote.

From that, I had derived hope. Wicked, monstrous hope. I came by it honestly.

Michael's parents, wonderful people, divorced when they were in their twenties, but married each other again three years later. They've been together now for more than fifty years. I believed that, like his parents, Michael and I were destined to be together. He just needed a little more time than I did to lick his wounds.

It didn't occur to me that Michael might just be trying to keep me placid for the upcoming divorce hearing, in which I would have to tell the judge that yes, our financial agreement was fair.

The day of the hearing arrives, and we both show up on time. We sit in the back row together; silently, awkwardly. I tear up only once—when a gruff bailiff approaches and tells me to put away my *Runner's World* magazine. Not being a frequent visitor to courtrooms, I hadn't known you aren't allowed to read there.

Three marriages dissolve before ours. When our turn comes, we walk up to the front. The judge asks if our marriage is unfixably broken, we both quietly say, "Yes," and it's over. We walk down the courtroom aisle side by side. No one throws rice.

It's more over than I thought.

A few weeks later, on Thanksgiving, after an awkward dinner together as a family, Michael tells me he is seeing someone, and he plans to introduce her to the kids. "It's not serious or anything," he says. "I just didn't want you to hear it from them."

I am unfazed. We just had Thanksgiving dinner together and will be together again on Christmas morning. Besides, a man who's been married for eighteen years, then wakes up divorced, in the Land of Wild Things, must feel the need to say "Let the wild rumpus start!" I understand this. He has some things to get out of his system before returning to us. We can wait.

A few months pass, and they're still not out of his system.

I cry to his sister, another mother of four, on the phone. "Tell him how you feel," she urges.

So I write him a four-page, single-spaced letter, probably the most beautiful thing I've ever composed.

It's true, I write, the last year we lived together was a made-for-TV drama called *Angry Man on the Couch*. But before that, we'd had sixteen mostly good years, and four great children, and a rich and complicated history that began in high school. Our lives, our families are forever entwined. We are bound by blood, oath, and IHOP. We were—we *are*—so much more than the events of the past three years, I write.

A friend of mine, miserable and confused, is considering leaving her husband. A mutual friend of ours pleads for their marriage. "I know you're having a terrible time now, but you have to hang on. Never give up. Never, ever give up. Keep telling yourself that. This will pass. It seems long and hard now, but it will pass, and you will forget. In twenty years, when you are sitting on the couch together, with grandchildren in your lap, you will be *so* glad you stayed."

My friend is still married. She is so glad she stayed. I am glad for her. I want to be glad for me.

I mail the letter and wait. Two days pass, then three, then four, without a response from Michael. This can't be good. If he misses us like we miss him, he would have come over the moment he opened my letter.

Still, I hope. *Dum spiro spero.*

Our estrangement, separation, and divorce had always seemed like a bad dream, a bitter vapor of sleep. Blindly, dumbly, we'd taken a wrong turn. But during our separation, the fog had cleared, and now we could see our way back, correct our dangerous course. Travel the straight and narrow path again. The two of us. The six of us, all holding hands.

Writing that letter felt right, one sure thing in this new life that felt so wrong, that was requiring I possess a bottle of Wellbutrin. I got the message, God. When you do wrong things, things go badly. When you do the right things, things go well. Everything is going to be okay now.

Late Sunday afternoon. I'm raking the paddock and the children are tossing a Frisbee in the backyard when Michael's Jeep pulls into the driveway, unannounced. He gets out, walks over to the barn, and holds out a Dunkin' Donuts cup.

"Long time, no talk," he says. "Could you use one of these?"

When we were married, Michael would often surprise me with a cappuccino or latte, indulging my lifelong quest for the perfect cup of coffee. This is a very good sign.

I set down the rake, wipe my hands on my jeans, and walk over to the gate where he stands. "Thanks," I say, and take the cup, grateful to have something to do with my hands. This is the father of my children, a man I've known since I was seventeen, but I am trembling. Michael and I haven't had a relaxed, genial conversation in nearly two years.

"We should talk," he says, and I nod.

But I gesture to my dirty boots and stained jeans. "I can't right now. I've got to finish cleaning the paddock, and then we're going to church."

We both look over to where our children are romping about the yard; they haven't spotted him yet.

"Okay, how about tomorrow, after the show?"

"Okay," I say, "tomorrow." I pick up my rake and watch as he walks over to the children, who shriek joyfully and run to him when they see him. He looks different. Although he's always been slender, he's lost weight and seems sort of tanned, even though as long as I've known him, his ruddy Celtic skin only burns in the sun.

He is wearing new blue jeans and a green pullover shirt that looks like it came from Lord & Taylor, not Target, where we usually shopped. He hugs the kids, and we wave as he drives away.

The next morning, I am whistling while I fry bacon and scramble the eggs. "Don't read anything into this," I tell my teen daughter when she sits down on a stool at the island, "but your father and I are having coffee this afternoon, and I need you to watch the little kids."

"Ooh la la," Alex says, grinning. "Do you need me to do something with your hair?"

Then Katherine bounds in, having overheard the conversation, and asks excitedly if we are going to get "undivorced."

"Oh, no, honey, don't think that," I say to her, even though that's *exactly* what I'm thinking. "We're just having coffee and are going to talk for a while."

Despite my denials, there is electricity at breakfast, a hum of excitement and hope.

Later that day, it goes out.

Michael is not, in fact, interested in an undivorce, but in making our divorce more permanent.

He tells me this after listening to me plead for our marriage for an hour, under a cluster of tall pine trees in a state park I often run through.

"I don't want to hurt you. I don't even want to have this conversation," he said. "But it's dead. There is no 'us' anymore."

When Katherine got off the bus that afternoon, she had run down the driveway, leapt in my arms, and joyfully said, "We've got to make you pretty for Daddy!" She had brushed my hair and chose the clothes I was wearing: a short black skirt and a black, V-necked tee.

I now pull the shirt to my face, exposing my pale, mottled stomach, to unprettily wipe away my tears.

We'd talked for an hour, getting nowhere, just like our conversations of the past two years. The sun will be going down soon.

I turn toward the park entrance, and, trying to be upbeat through my tears, say, "Well, we've got a five-minute walk to the car. Any parting words?"

That's when he says it, to my back.

"We're getting married in November."

Looking back on that horrible moment, I see now I should have run.

I should have turned my back, slipped off my sandals, threw them at him, and run off, as fast as I could. Run all the way around the reservoir. Down the rocky forest trails, followed them to where they end in town.

I should have run past the Ashland train station, the Dairy Queen. Past Framingham Center, and the Brazilian buffet where the six of us used to eat, and past Natick Center, Wellesley College, all the way to Heartbreak Hill. I should have run until my feet were bruised and bleeding. Run until my toenails fell off.

Then, only then, could I have calmly returned home, collected the kids, and driven the seventeen hours to South Carolina, where people love me.

These are the three most popular words of divorcées: shoulda, woulda, coulda.

I should have run. Instead, I crumple.

I sink to my knees, sobbing, my fingers raking the bark of a sympathetic oak tree.

Michael stops for a moment and looks hesitant, but then walks off, leaving me howling and hugging the tree.

Blindly, I dig in my skirt pocket, find my cell phone, and punch ICE—"in case of emergency"—my mother. When she answers, I'm gasping between sobs.

"He's getting *married*," I wail. "I thought we were going to get back together, but they're getting *married*."

I have to repeat this three times, because she cannot understand what I'm saying. She later tells Michael's mother that, because I was so hysterical, she at first thought someone had died.

Not somebody. Something.

Hope, that wicked, monstrous beast. Forever, may it burn in hell.

I tell my mother I'll call her later, when I'm more composed, then sob under the tree until my pretty black T-shirt is soaked. Then I collect myself, walk the mile back home, and enter a brief period of rage.

Well, okay, maybe six months is not brief, strictly speaking. But personally, I think the circumstances warrant six years. I cut it short only to preserve what remains of my mental health.

But grief persists, the sole survivor in Shoulda-Woulda-Coulda Land, and I expect it to intensify as the wedding approaches. This is why I still hang on to my bottle of happy pills, hidden under my Miraclesuit tummy-control swimsuits. Just in case I need the pills (or the swimsuits) if tears flood the basement someday. It's also why I listen when my coach tells me to hurt harder. And it's why I'm not happy, but grateful, to have a race for which to train.

twenty

Tired Is Not an Option

Worst. Run. Ever.

That's today.

The first half a mile is always a struggle, the violent ejection of inertia, but today's run is horrible from the first step to the last. My legs were dead on departure, dead on arrival. Clearly, I've developed Chronic Fatigue Syndrome. Or polio, some strain that overcomes the vaccinations of childhood. Maybe you *can* run yourself into the ground.

I run because I have no choice. But every step is despairing. During the night, some rude imp unscrewed my legs and filled them with concrete. I can no longer run. From now on, I will only shuffle.

But—I shuffle four and a half miles. That's something, isn't it? I comfort myself with platitudes as I sprawl on the moss-covered stones of the patio and lift a knee to stretch. I'm so tired. Physically tired, emotionally tired, spiritually tired. No one has ever been more tired than me. It's a weariness that comes not just from physical exhaustion, but the abandonment of hope. I rise and look over at an empty paddock. The gate is ajar. There are no donkeys.

I've given Foggy and Jo-Jo away.

After the narrowly averted Donkeygeddon, there'd been two more

169

instances of inadvertent freedom. Both involved human error—stalls and doors left open carelessly. These are not crazed beasts breaking down fences and bolting away. But they're no dummies, either. Given the opportunity to seek greener pastures, they don't wait to ask my permission.

The last two times the donkeys got out, they kept off the road and away from school buses, and instead took a leisurely tour of neighborhood yards. They had a delightful time. The snacks were wonderful. It was the Donkey Tour of Homes, like the human ones sponsored by the Junior League or the Homebuilders' Association.

I found out they were gone like I usually do. A strange car pulled into the driveway, and someone got out and walked around the yard, and when I yelled out the window, "May I help you?" I heard the five most terrifying words on Earth:

Do you have two donkeys?

A vow: Next time, I'm saying, "Why, no! Only cats."

See, I *am* capable of learning.

But before I figured this out, I would look over at the now empty paddock, race out the door and collect their halters and lead ropes, and head off to wherever they were.

Later, the children and I will buy blueberry pies from Out Post, the local turkey farm, and make deliveries, meekly seeking absolution for nibbled shrubs and trampled grass. If the damage is bad enough, Katherine will make a card saying "We are sorry the donkeys ate your yard." But the pies usually do the trick. These pies are so good that sometimes I wonder if people don't sneak over to my house and let the donkeys out when I'm not looking, hoping they'll get a free pie.

Everyone's been nice so far, even the family that had just seeded their lawn. Still, I worry so much about the staggering liabilities under my care. All of them, the hooved, pawed, and footed. At night, I climb in bed and, and instead of enjoying the luxury of having a California king all to myself, I am listening when I should be sleeping. Listening for anyone still awake. Listening for anything in trouble.

Blogger Glennon Melton writes that putting young children to bed is a game of Whack-a-Mole; kids pop up and down with the flimsiest of excuses. Mine request water, kisses, bandages, signatures on forgotten school papers, and the occasional relocation of spiders until the point at which my eyes narrow menacingly and I hiss not to approach me again unless someone is bleeding. And a few drops of blood do not count. They better need a transfusion.

At that point, the house usually falls silent.

But even then, I remain awake, listening for sounds from the barn. I've never had such an emergency—knock on inch-and-a-half-thick raw pine fencing—but breakouts happen. And colic. And founder, and broken limbs. Anything can happen when five-hundred-pound farm animals are involved, and the laws of Murphy being what they are, anything is more likely to happen when there's only one adult on the premises.

Another casualty of divorce is satisfying, revitalizing REM sleep. Single parents sleep, yes, but never too deeply. I've read that, in packs of wild mammals, one animal always sleeps lightly, poised to spring into action if danger threatens the tribe. The adults of the pack take turns being the half-drowsing watchman so the others can rest.

I think this happens in human packs, too. In well functioning families, two parents become one creature, akin to the pushmi-pul-lyu in *The Story of Doctor Dolittle*. In Hugh Lofting's classic children's book, the pushmi-pullyu has two heads, one on either end. When one end is awake, the other is sleeping, so the beast—or at least some part of him—is always alert. A mother and father working together to raise kids operate much like this; when one wearies or despairs, the other takes over.

Divorce slays this vital beast, the parental pushmi-pullyu. And like the Thane of Glamis, it murders sleep, at least for the custodial parent. Somewhere else, the non-custodial parent snores ecstatically, without care.

Being the custodial parent, the primary stall mucker, and a compulsory runner, I am tired all the time. I am tired of being tired, and tired of worrying about alarming noises in the night, and tired of wondering where to find the money for next week's hay, and tired of envisioning the lawsuits that will be visited upon me if Foggy crashes into a school bus the next time he escapes if I don't happen to be coming around the corner on my bike.

It's time for Foggy to go. Foggy and Jo-Jo. The both of them.

I wish I could sell them, because we need the money, but donkeys have virtually no value in America right now. In Greece, they're widely used for transportation, and in Africa, people eat barbecued donkey meat, but here, excess horses are a national problem; excess donkeys even more so. There is no market for unskilled donkeys, and Foggy and Jo-Jo are as unskilled as they come.

The other thing is, perhaps foolishly, I'm determined to keep them together. I couldn't keep my own marriage intact, but I have vowed I will not separate these two. Neither had known another donkey other than their mothers; after weaning, they'd spent their early years as companions to horses. When they first saw each other, they sniffed each other and brayed enthusiastically, and they remain crazily besotted in love. They even eat their hay together, heads side by side. I'm not splitting them up. Foggy and Jo-Jo stay together.

That said, Foggy, you know, has issues.

Not many people in this world want a Foggy.

But incredibly, after a few weeks of searching, I find one who does. Nancy lives an hour away with her three horses—two of which cannot be ridden, because they, like Foggy, have issues. But she loves her problem ponies and has vowed they can live out the rest of their lives on her farm.

I love this woman immediately.

Nancy is looking for donkeys she can train for children's birthday parties. Jo-Jo is already there; she is calm and obedient, can be ridden, and is tolerant of zany party hats. Foggy is not tolerant of anything but Jo-Jo, but Nancy figures he'll come around with time and training.

Off they go.

There is weeping and gnashing of teeth. Katherine posts signs all over the house that say, SAVE THE DONKEYS! My oldest son writes an essay for English class in which he says the barn, once the liveliest place he knew, has become the most dead.

I miss them, too. But I don't miss the work. I don't miss having to get up to throw hay and shovel manure at seven o'clock on Sunday mornings when the kids are with their dad and I could be sleeping. I don't miss the endless trips to take soiled, rancid bedding to a dump fifteen minutes away. I don't miss the responsibility. I don't miss not being able to leave my house for more than five hours at a time.

I do, however, miss the donkeys. Like my son predicted, the barn is cold and forlorn. Dead like my legs feel today.

But I had to do it. I had to let them go. Can't anyone see how tired I am?

I hear a voice, curt and succinct.

Tired is not an option.

Oh, go away.

Tired means you've done too much. Tired means you're at your limit. Tired means time to rest, to do less.

Rest, yes. For a while. Then you take on, not less, but more.

Progressive overload. I know exactly what Pre means. And where he heard it first.

Take a primitive organism, say a freshman. Make it lift, or jump or run. Let it rest. What happens? A little miracle. It gets a little better. It gets a little stronger, or faster or more enduring. That's all training is. Stress. Recover. Improve.

Bill Bowerman. Trainer of immortals, popping his head in again.

I want to play Whack-a-Coach.

But I know. The problem with most people is, they quit after they rest. They don't have the will, or the guts, to keep adding to the load. To see how much they can hoist.

It's simple, really: To make something easy, make it harder.

I thought one kid was a lot of work until I had two. I thought two kids were a lot of work until I had four. I thought four kids were a lot of work until I got divorced. Now, having four kids in a two-parent family would seem like a breeze.

Lift, jump, or run.

I choose to run.

And of course—because in this world, even the dead won't go away—of course, the donkeys will be back.

In a couple of months, I will get an email from Nancy, saying that Jo-Jo isn't getting along with her horses. I will be skeptical of this. She's being nice. I think the problem is Foggy.

It won't matter. She will want to bring them back, right away.

It will be the middle of January in New England. There will be three feet of snow in the paddock, and we will have no hay, and the frost-free spigot will be broken and frozen, and we will have to haul water from the kitchen, and shovel manure six times a day, and we will all be surprised by our joy. It will be a happy homecoming. One that I'd wished to have with my children's father, but barring that circumstance, donkeys will do.

The donkeys will come home, and they won't seem unhappy about it, and the barn will be lit and alive again, even in the dead, icy stillness of winter.

I will still be tired, and they will still be too much work, but I know the solution now. There is a way to make the care of donkeys seem easy, and when the time comes, we'll do it.

We'll get a dog. A high-energy dog, a border collie, that wakes at six and has to be run every hour.

To make things easy, make them harder.

Meanwhile, my dead legs revive. There's no polio, of course. Just stress, recovery, and improvement.

Everyone's dead now and then. Doesn't mean we won't, in an instant, find a way to vault back to life.

twenty-one

How Nike Made Me a Terrorist

When you look like me, going through airport security is usually no big deal.

Blond hair, green eyes, and a waist with the circumference of an extra-large pizza make me an unlikely candidate for in-flight disruption. Add the usual presence of a kid—or two, or four—and me shuffling through the gauntlet of grim screeners is about as interesting as watching paint dry.

Until Nike+ made me a terrorist.

True story.

Earlier this year, I flew to South Carolina for a wedding, leaving the children behind with their dad. Since it's February, I plan to stay an extra day to indulge in a pleasure unavailable to New England runners in the winter: streets without snow, ice, or salt. I figure it's a good time to build up my mileage and measure it accurately with a new gadget that Santa had brought.

Not to be a shill for Nike (particularly since Alberto Salazar works there), but after the iPod, Nike+ is the greater thing ever. For thirty dollars, you buy a little oval sensor that fits in a Nike+ shoe. Then you attach the receiver to your iPod, and off you go, the smart little sensor measuring your every step.

At the end of the run, your iPod tells you how far you went, how fast you ran, and how many calories you burned. Sometimes, on a good day, Lance Armstrong will tell you it was your fastest mile ever!

It is, quite possibly, the best thing to be had for thirty dollars in the US marketplace.

Well, ninety dollars actually, since twice I've had to buy a new one. The receiver's battery can't be replaced, so when it wears out, you've got to buy another. But it's like running in general. Once you're hooked, you don't mind the occasional trifling indignity.

But you always want to know how far you've run.

Want to make small talk with a runner? Ask her to tell you about her first mile. I remember mine: It was from my front yard to the stop sign on my beloved Syrup Mill Road, about six months after I started running. It was just one mile without stopping, but I was so tired and happy at the end, I felt like I'd run to the moon.

I knew it was exactly a mile because I'd measured it on my car odometer—the only way I could measure my mileage until Nike+ came along. With the sensor in my shoe, I could measure not only my miles on the road, but also my detours through trails and meadows, and my runs down the beach.

Nike+ made every mile count. For me, it was life-changing stuff.

Of course, you can also use it for other things, such as connecting with fellow runners on the Nike website, or identifying on which day of the week you run most (Wednesday! Who knew?). But my mileage is what I care about most.

I'm also increasingly interested in my pace, which, as of yesterday, ten minutes, thirty-one seconds per mile, which I achieved on a 3.73-mile run. This is not great. But it's better than the 10:41 pace at which I'd last run this route, and the 11:10 pace at which I'd started training for Kiawah.

Not that I'm getting obsessive about this stuff, or anything.

But back to my new career as a terrorist.

I read once that you should always wear athletic shoes on a plane, in case you ever need to sprint away from flames or shiver on a wing in the Hudson River. So I enter the security line at Charleston International Airport, clutching my ID, boarding pass and Nike shoes.

My iPod and the receiver are packed in my check-on bag, but the sensor with which they communicate is still tucked in the sole of my left shoe. (Cue ominous music here.)

I smile and make small talk as the line snakes along, and, this being the South, the agents smile and make small talk back at me. Until the plastic trays containing my laptop and shoes go through the scanner, and a loud buzzer sounds.

"Wait here," the agent says, suddenly not smiling.

I step aside while she put my trays on the front of the belt again.

They begin to move, and again, the buzzer goes off.

"Ma'am, will you step out of line, please?"

I comply, bewildered.

I'd checked a bag, and so all I am carrying is my purse, a book, a laptop, and a phone. I know I have no liquids or gels; I'd gone through my purse and tossed all that before leaving the hotel.

But it isn't my purse attracting the scrutiny of the agent. It's my running shoes.

As a threat to my fellow travelers, I am now apparently approaching Code Red.

Backup is summoned.

Soon three officers cluster around my running shoes, while I stand there in socks, mortified. Apparently, bad smells set off airport security alarms. In the future, I will travel in the company of Dr. Scholl's Odor Destroyers foot spray.

But they're not smelling my shoes. They're squinting at them. Holding them up to a light.

I see the mug shot. Mother of Four, Accused Shoe Bomber. The first terrorist is the family. My mother will be so proud. Maybe I stepped on some TNT on the way here.

Suddenly, one of the officers peels back the shoe liner, exposing my Nike+ sensor.

"Oh, so that's the problem," I say and laugh in relief.

The TSA agents do not laugh. They ignore me. One pries the sensor out of the shoe and holds it at eye level. The others step back, anticipating a detonation.

I stop laughing. These guys are humorless. They're probably all wearing New Balance.

I try again. "It's Nike+. It's for my iPod. It's a little sensor that measures my mileage when I'm running."

The Sole Train, all three of them, turn to look at me. They look at my face. Their gazes drop to my waist. Then my hips. My shoeless feet.

Yeah, right, I can see them thinking.

And why, *exactly, do you want the Runner's Revenge massage?*

Adeptly, they defuse my relief. Then they turn and hunch again over the evil transponder with which I am clearly planning to blow up an airplane.

Meanwhile, other passengers—many of whom look more dangerous than me—are passing through security unmolested. A few grin at me. I stand there miserably, thinking of the comedian Jeff Dunham while meekly awaiting arrest.

Dunham is a ventriloquist whose puppets include a turban-wearing skeleton named "Achmed the Dead Terrorist."

Achmed blew himself up while trying to kill innocents. He now spends eternity shrieking "I kill you" and toggling his bushy eyebrows to the amusement of the infidels around him, who consider him what he is: a joke.

I don't know who is more frightening, Achmed the Dead Terrorist, or me. However, because I would like to get back to Boston tonight, I keep this thought to myself.

Eventually, the SWAT team determines the little piece of plastic in my shoe is unlikely to down a 737. From the looks on their faces, however, they're still not convinced I'm a runner. Maybe they think I picked up these shoes, transponder in place, at the Salvation Army. Or I'm pretending to be a runner for a new Sacha Baron Cohen film.

Still eyeing me with suspicion, a TSA agent hands me my shoes, purse, and laptop. I kneel to lace my shoes and then have to sprint to get to the gate on time. Taking my seat on the plane, I look down at my shoes and think, *Will I ever look like my tribe?*

I worry that I do, and my real tribe can be found at Walmart on a Saturday night.

I go there sometimes to buy groceries and gardening supplies, and to confirm that the author of *People of Walmart* is an evil genius.

Not that I have anything against Walmart. Au contraire. I *vacation* at Walmart.

I swear I don't make this stuff up.

I met my best friend, Diane, when I worked for the afternoon newspaper. It was right about the time I started to run. She is my *other* reliable source of joy, one that doesn't require nearly as much exertion. In fact, Diane and my grandmother share the same philosophy on my sport. It is this: *Jim Fixx died while running, ergo, running kills.* I once coaxed Diane into walking the Cooper River Bridge Run with me; her first, and last, 10K.

Anyway, not long after we both got married, Diane up and left, took a job at a newspaper in Ohio, her home state. To ensure we didn't lose touch (there was no Facebook then), we decided to meet—with another friend—once or twice a year at a state park in West Virginia. It's where Dr. Sheehan introduced me to Pre.

We've been doing this now for almost as long as I was married. So long that once, the staff put up a sign that said WELCOME, DIANE, JENNIFER AND CAROL! We pass the days in the happy stupor of long-marrieds: eating, sleeping, talking about the kids and the weather, and, for excitement, shopping at the Bluefield Walmart.

Yes, it's true. Each year, I travel 750 miles to shop at the Walmart in West Virginia. There have been times—I'm ashamed to admit it—we've been twice. In one day.

But, understand, it's only because there's no IHOP.

I dream of being an international distance runner, competing in marathons in Zurich, Hamburg, and Madrid. But no. I'm too tired and too broke to even get to the Famous Idaho Potato Marathon in Boise.

I would say I'm hopelessly bourgeois, but helplessly redneck is probably close to the truth.

I might be a redneck, not only because I consider Walmart a vacation destination, but because I run with a second-generation iPod strapped to my arm. Also, I own, and sometimes use, a heart-rate monitor even though an eleven-minute miler needs a heart-rate monitor like a single mother of four needs a donkey.

I am running white trash, a smashed Gatorade cup on the sidelines of life.

It's a good thing Alberto Salazar didn't offer to train me because he wouldn't have put up with my ever-present iPod. World-class marathoners don't listen to music while they train. Naturally fast, they don't need the artificial pep Nickleback provides. And since they're not blasting music in their ears, they can monitor their own heart rates with, say, their senses. A hundred-dollar Polar FT4 would only add weight to their chests and slow them down.

Even for plodders like me, the experts frown at listening to music on a run. It's not safe. You can't hear a car coming up behind you, let alone two donkeys and a school bus.

Moreover, wearing an armband, an iPod, and earbuds just looks kind of sissy. It's like wearing leg warmers or one of those terry sweatbands that were so popular in the 1980s. It's an announcement to all lookers: *It's Amateur Hour!*

And if an iPod strapped to my arm looks silly now, imagine how cool I looked twenty years ago, when all we had were Walkmans, those Eggo-sized cassette players we had to carry. Carrying one of those was like running with a cantaloupe.

But I did it then, and run with an iPod today for the same reason my hero George Sheehan drank coffee: It gets me out the door. And once out there, it makes me feel like I'm dancing.

Running with an MP3 player is dancing for people too self-conscious to dance.

But I'm not stupid about it. If I'm on the road, I only use one earbud, so I can hear eighteen-wheelers rumbling up behind me. The volume is never loud unless I'm on a track or out in the woods.

In 2007, USA Track & Field, which governs racing in this country, banned portable music devices in its sanctioned events, but later amended the ban to apply only to top contenders. For the USATF, safety was the issue. It's hard enough avoiding collisions with other racers when you're *not* wearing headphones.

I'd never use an iPod in a race, not only because they're often forbidden, but because it would take away from the experience. Why run in a group if you're only going to be present in your head? If anyone yells, "Wow, look at that endomorph go!" I want to be able to hear it.

But day in and day out, music elevates my run. It can almost be an opiate when you're training, lessening the perception of discomfort by about 10 percent, according to Costas Karageorghis, a sports psychologist quoted in *Runner's World*.

Karageorghis describes top competitors as "associates," athletes in tune with their breathing, heart rate, and muscular tension while they work out. "Dissociators" are people who want to be distracted from the effort at hand. People like me.

But I don't see this as proof that I'm not a competitor. Galen Rupp would dissociate, too, if his thighs made as much noise as mine do.

twenty-two

The Interment of Hope

It is one month until my race, and three days until Michael's wedding. I am driving eleven hours to West Virginia to meet Diane at Pipestem Resort State Park, where, upon arrival, my car will break down.

This must be some cosmic joke. My Jeep breaks down, for the first time, on the weekend of my former husband's wedding? Stranding me a thousand miles from home?

To add to the surreal horror story that is my life, the tow-truck driver, when he arrives an hour late, is named Cleatus.

Cleatus is not a Shirtless Wonder. Diane and I are relieved he has his shirt on.

Cleatus loads the Jeep on the back of his truck and clucks sympathetically, the insincere vocalizing of someone who's sorry about your misfortune—but not really, because it's putting a hundred bucks in his pocket. He looks curiously at my red, swollen eyes, but has the good sense not to ask who died.

Diane arrived at Pipestem with art supplies, a sewing machine, a blender, tequila, and an extra-large bottle of Kahlúa. If she cannot erase my pain, she is prepared to drown it, and then we will craft ourselves into oblivion.

At home, my former in-laws are arriving for the wedding. Some of them will be staying in my house. Michael's best friend, the best man at our wedding, will be there.

At our rehearsal dinner eighteen years ago, he gave a toast and accidentally called me Gina, the name of Michael's first wife.

I fervently hope his toast tonight is to Michael and Jennifer.

I fervently hope there's a karma train out there.

Only, the wedding, of course, isn't going to happen. At any time, Michael is going to wake up from *his* bad dream, slap his forehead, and say, "My God, what I have done?" He will speed to the airport, talk his way onto a flight, and soon be banging on the door at my cabin, where he will find Diane and me drooling Kahlúa and painting hieroglyphics on the cabin floor.

We will welcome him. We believe in redemption. We believe in shepherds who leave the flock to search for a single lost sheep.

In her memoir *Bread of Angels,* Stephanie Saldaña, an American Christian, teaches a class of Muslim girls in Syria, and they delight in the similarities of each faith's version of the tale. For Muslims, it's not a lost sheep, but a camel.

The Koran says, "Allah is more pleased with the repentance of His servant than a person who has his camel in a waterless desert, carrying his provision of food and drink, and it is lost. He, having lost all hopes of getting it back, lies down in the shade and is disappointed about his camel, when, all of a sudden, he finds that camel standing before him."

I wish for my camel.

But my Saturday night will be about a horse. Diane and I have decided to spend the three-hour agony of the wedding watching a movie, *Secretariat*. Since I've loved horses since childhood, this film will ground me, keep me in touch with the things that matter most in my life.

Saturday dawns cloudy and grim. My driveway is vacant; my eyes are swollen and sore. It is a day I didn't really believe would come. But as of today, I no longer possess hope.

I miss it.

I still hope vaguely, of course, for the future. But I've come to believe that short-term hope, the kind you need the most, never seems to deliver.

Surely you know. Nobody ever knocks on the door when you're on your knees sobbing in the dark. The phone doesn't ring. Flowers aren't delivered. No ambulance drives by when you're trapped under your car.

The blackest moments of our lives always, always remain black. Surely, this has to mean something. Otherwise, the sheer odds of living would guarantee that, on at least one occasion, someone would accidentally stumble in and rescue you, if life is as random, as senseless, as the atheists say.

But they never do.

I still can't accept the reality that, for perhaps the first time in my life, I've done everything right—followed my compass, played by the rules, worked out at 85 percent of my maximum heart rate—and still, the outcome has turned out so badly.

The past few years have been horrible. I've visited the depths. But I see the ways in which I'm a better person for it. I'm a better parent, more attentive and expressive of my love for my kids. Having lost so much, I am grateful for the relationships that remain. I call my mother and grandmother more often. I put more effort into my relationships with my girlfriends.

Physically, I've never been stronger. I am running well, riding a bike and a horse and occasionally swimming, exerting myself to exhaustion almost daily and eating no more than usual.

And yet I still weigh exactly the same as I did last year.

I look back on all the suffering of the past three years, physical and emotional, and I see no purpose in any of it—no payoff, no vision, however distant, of how any of this pain could be worth it, for me or my kids.

I think of the Ghost of Christmas Yet to Come standing over the cowering Scrooge, Scrooge pleading for the chance to learn from his ghastly visitors.

"Spirit," he cried, tight clutching at its robe. "Hear me. I am not the man I was. I will not be the man I must have been for this intercourse. Why show me this if I am past all hope?"

Scrooge lives, he born of fiction.

Pre, and my marriage, born of reality, do not.

I make a list of the good things. I'm healthy, ridiculously so. The kids are thriving; so are the donkeys. I have a home, at least for ten more years. We haven't declared bankruptcy yet. Even at my most miserable, I've never once wished I were dead.

Then I think of something curious. Even though I must have an eating disorder (surely a thirty-year diet without losing weight qualifies as an eating disorder), even at my most miserable, I didn't *gain* any weight.

That's something, I think.

If I were really hopeless, wouldn't I have spent the past three years immersed in a giant tub of vanilla ice cream?

Instead, I've been out training. Kicking ass, my own. Okay, well, yeah, with an invisible coach, with imaginary friends, but still.

There are theories that our bodies all have weight set points, plateaus at which the body settles and won't depart without significant, sustained effort. Anecdotally, I've seen this to be true in my own life.

Down or up, my weight always seems to settle on something ending in three. 203. 183. 153. I get to a decade ending in three, and there I hover. I'll go up a few, down a few, depending on how much I run, and how much money I have. (More money means more salmon, which means lost weight.) But I always seem to plateau around the three.

Maybe I'm afraid of success. Maybe I get close to another, lower decade on the scale, and continually sabotage myself to keep myself from getting there.

But scientists who study set-point theory say there may be other, more comforting factors at work.

Researchers at the Massachusetts Institute for Technology say the set point remains constant because the body has its own intelligence, and knows more about its fat stores than the conscious mind.

The body intelligent surmises the weight at which we will be most energetic and optimistic. It understands that when aggressively dieting, we can feel lethargic, so it works to keep us at set point, to keep our mood and our weight stable. Our bodies, our minds, work together to protect each other, to care for their own. Plateaus are good, of body and mind. The body craves stability, yes?

Or not. Plateaus keep me from being three hundred pounds. But they also keep me from being 138.

A body at rest remains at rest.

I don't want to be at rest. I'd rather hurt and be active than be pain-free and inert. I am the spiritual child of George Sheehan, who loved to quote William James: "The strenuous life tastes best."

For three years, I've been looking for a sign to hang over my bed, to replace the one that formerly hung there that said ALWAYS KISS ME GOODNIGHT.

When Michael moved out, I donated it to the Salvation Army thrift shop, where some lucky shopper probably bought it for a buck. I thought I'd find something more appropriate to hang there, so I could quickly cover up the reproachful vacant screws.

Frank Lloyd Wright carved LIFE IS TRUTH over the mantel at his Illinois home a century ago. That doesn't work so well for me, given that much of my life right now is illusion.

But I can't seem to find the right sign. Everything I see in stores and catalogs is vapid and hoary.

LIVE! LAUGH! LOVE!

LIVE IT! DREAM IT! DO IT!

WHAT IF THE HOKEY POKEY IS WHAT IT'S ALL ABOUT?

These would certainly fill the space, but they're not me. Neither are ALL BECAUSE TWO PEOPLE FELL IN LOVE and IT'S NOT TOO LATE TO HAVE A HAPPY ENDING.

Uh, clearly, it is.

At least, it will be, later today.

BE NICE OR LEAVE seems appropriate, but late. LIFE'S SHORT, EAT

COOKIES, too revealing. A PRINCESS SLEEPS HERE does as much for my future prospects as my old radio identity "The Warden."

And the most popular sign of all throws me into a rage. IT IS WHAT IT IS.

No, dammit, it's not. It doesn't have to be.

You don't *have* to stay broken, divorced, broke, fat. You don't *have* to stay at rest. That's what I believe.

I believe it passionately. I truly do. Even though I'm broken, divorced, broke, fat.

But I'm never at rest. I won't be today. I run seven miles, to the end of the road and back, to dull the pain. I am slow, breathe heavily, and stop to walk often. No personal records for me today.

But I finish.

As I shower and numbly dress for the movie, I think. *Maybe sometimes, a plateau is progress. Maybe sometimes not going backward is going forward enough. Maybe a body at rest needs a rest.*

I look over to Pre, expecting a frown, but he is silent. I wait for a rebuttal, a challenge. Then, soberly, he nods.

twenty-three

Lady Madonna

In Greek mythology, the fearsome Sphinx asked a question of travelers: What goes on four legs in the morning, two legs at noon, and three legs in the evening?

Oedipus knew the answer was "man." First, we are crawling babies, on all fours. Then we are sure-footed, two-legged adults. Then, finally, we are seasoned citizens, aided by our third "legs"—canes.

Well, Oedipus lived a long time ago.

I'm old enough to glimpse the end of my journey, but young enough to be optimistic about it. Enabling that wretched hope is a nun.

Sister Madonna Buder is an eighty-year-old triathlete, whose book *The Grace to Race* I came upon a few days ago.

In it, I learned she was a child of privilege: a gorgeous debutante who was a competitive equestrian and a model; well traveled, well educated, and well loved, both by her family and by a parade of ardent suitors. It was astonishing enough that, back in 1956, she turned her back on worldly pleasures and took vows to become a nun. But her story became even more compelling when, at the age of forty-eight—my age now—she went for her first run, at the suggestion of a priest.

Sister Madonna, a rat like us, was immediately hooked on running, and later took up cycling and swimming. She now sets age records as a triathlete. When she's not traveling the world competing, she grows her own salad greens, like Pre, and runs to Mass every day.

Sister Madonna says anyone can run. "A lot of people are their own worst enemies. When they start thinking about their age, they say, 'Oh, this hurts, that hurts, I can't do this, I can't do that.' Well, so what?" she writes. "When you were a kid, you didn't bother about what hurt, you just went out and did it."

I'm three-quarters through the book, and she's already broken her hip, ribs, and both elbows, and finished an Ironman competition (2.4-mile swim, 112-mile bike ride, and a full marathon) with two broken toes.

She's run the Boston Marathon, right past me—me, who is a little more than half her age.

She shames me, even more than my coach. But, like Pre, she also inspires. Because lately, I've been feeling my age.

When Michael first told me he was dating, I assumed he was seeing someone close to our age. When I learned the girlfriend was thirty-three, I was unprepared for how that news made me feel.

I've never been the kind of woman who obsessed about age. When I turned thirty, I was pregnant, and when I turned forty, I was pregnant, and being pregnant, no matter how old you are, makes you feel young. Only young women have babies, right?

Even as the forties advanced, I've never lied about my age. I always give it freely when asked. Sometimes I give it even when I'm not asked, in newspaper articles I write.

But suddenly, replaced by someone fifteen years my junior, a woman without stretch marks and crow's-feet, my age became some-thing sensitive and raw. For the first time, I became embarrassed by my age, which is not so much a number, or the year I was born, but seems the sum of my sun-weathered face.

Fat and scarred as it may be, my body still seems young—to me, anyway. After a long run, I take a bath and lie back in the water, rest-ing my head on rim of the tub. Doing this, I stretch and survey my body with a pleasure I don't feel when I'm trying on clothes.

Lapped by warm water, I am exquisitely weary, sublimely at peace, and fully conscious that at no time—not now, not twenty years ago—would Hugh Hefner seek to publish this image in his magazine.

In the tub, my body—*it floats high in water!*—still looks largely the same as it did twenty years ago. In good ways, as well as bad. It's still overfat, and dimpled with cellulite and streaked with thin purple lines. That is how it looks.

But this is how it *feels:* Strong. Able. Beautiful. I lift a leg in the air and am astounded at its reach. I marvel at how much I *like* this im-perfect limb attached to me. It seems such a useful and competent thing.

If I didn't *know* how old I am—and if I lived without mirrors and wasn't able to see my face—I would think I was thirty-three. Some-times, with enough coffee in me, and fresh off a good night's sleep, I might even venture an age closer to twenty-three. So much of what we believe about ourselves comes from equations that are not true. If X plus Y equals C, then Z. But what if X and Y are not true?

I question everything these days.

Maybe this is why I decided to consider my physical plateau of twenty years simply delayed progress. Plateaus are necessary. Desirable. Any frustration with them is just our insufficient comprehension of time.

I've heard it said that in the Bible's seven days of creation, we're still at midmorning of Day Seven.

I've heard it said that the Internet, though created in the 1970s, is, in the grand scheme of things, still on Day One.

Maybe we're all on Day One, in ways we don't even know. Maybe our time is not real time. Maybe there's more to *everything* than we know.

Over the weekend, I take my youngest kids roller skating, and since I know from reading James that the strenuous life tastes best, I join them in the rink. The three of us skate together, holding hands, Justin Bieber blasting from the loudspeakers. Mercifully, they're not yet at the age where it's an embarrassment to have their mother around. It's coming. I enjoy them while I can.

At one point, my senses under assault by pulsing disco lights and adolescent karaoke, I look around and realize I am the oldest person on skates. There are people older than me at the skating rink, sure. But they're all sitting, feet safely on the floor, in the café.

I'm the only woman old enough to be a grandmother and dumb enough to don Rollerblades.

Hallelujah.

There was a time when this would have bothered me, but no more. Now I aspire to be the oldest person in the game, Oedipus be damned.

There will be no cane for me.

Or if there is, I'll put it to use, club the Shirtless Wonders out of my way.

twenty-four

Shirtless Wonders

This is a real item from the weekly police blotter in my town:

5:18 P.M., Oct. 5. A Pond Street caller reported an unknown shirtless man walking around her back yard. [Officers] responded and located the man, who stated he was looking for his wife whom he had lost while jogging. His wife was located, and the couple was transported home.

Let's have a show of hands of anyone who thinks the *man* was lost, not the woman.

Sorry, guys.

But it's pretty obvious how this can happen. A Shirtless Wonder is having a good run, gets lost in himself, believes his own press, and doesn't notice he has left his poor, plodding wife in the dust. Then, without his wife—aka "sense of direction"—and sans a GPS, our poor Shirtless Wonder can't find his way back home.

Forgive my escalating levels of snark; I'm trying to keep it in check. Truthfully, in the worldwide family of runners, we generally all love one another, but just as in a real family, there's always someone who causes you to bristle reflexively. For me, it's the Shirtless Wonder, the haughty guy who wants you out of his way.

I hate to generalize, but let's.

Generally speaking, a Shirtless Wonder is tall and muscular, supremely proud of his physique and his speed. His commanding presence on the road demands that you look at him, but he would never make eye contact with you. (Exception: Occasionally, if wearing sunglasses, he will glance your way to confirm you are sufficiently admiring his abs.)

No matter how enthusiastically you salute him, no matter how obsequious you seem, a Shirtless Wonder will never wave back. As a matter of fact, he does own the road.

Women can be Shirtless Wonders, too, although they are not actually shirtless. Female Shirtless Wonders wear racer-back sports bras and are well tanned even in winter. They wear earrings, lipstick, and mascara to 10Ks.

Male or female, you can always identify Shirtless Wonders by the faint whiff of disdain that whirls around them. They condescend like a cloud.

I hate to name names, but let's. Gabriel Sherman is one. In his essay "Running with Slowpokes: How Newbies Ruined the Marathon" in *Slate* magazine, Sherman said running 26.2 miles in America has become "akin to joining a gym and then putzing around on the stationary bike."

"We feel good about creating the appearance of accomplishment, yet aren't willing to sacrifice for true gains," Sherman writes. "It's clear now that anyone can finish a marathon. Maybe it's time we raise our standards to see who can *run* one."

It was for people like Gabriel Sherman that I had two T-shirts made. One says, YEAH, YOU'RE FASTER THAN ME, BUT I'M ON MILE 10. The other: YEAH, YOU'RE FASTER THAN ME, BUT HAVE YOU HAD FOUR C-SECTIONS?

Sometimes I wear the C-section one when I race. Women always laugh. The Shirtless Wonders are never amused.

The Shirtless Wonders were out in full voice recently when Boston Marathon officials announced new registration procedures designed to ensure that the fastest qualifying runners get a spot in the race. Even in a recession, with a $130 entry fee, the 2011 marathon was filled to capacity eight hours after registration opened, making almost everyone irate.

"Real" runners, who had trained for years and qualified and met Boston's tough standards but didn't get in, howled indignantly that their slots were taken by amateurs running in tutus and Superman capes. There are "other" marathons for their kind, they sniffed.

And as much as I hate to side with a Shirtless Wonder, on this point, I kind of agree.

There are roughly 250 marathons in the United States each year, and most of them, including Chicago, do not require qualifying times. Boston has luster because it does.

To "run Boston"—the word *marathon* need never be used—is the ultimate test. It's the Super Bowl for distance runners. But because of that peculiar nature of road racing—all comers, all the time—people who would never demand inclusion in the Super Bowl, or the World Series, think they, too, have a God-given right to run Boston.

But the Boston Athletic Association is not a publicly held company. It's the BAA's race; they can shut out as many people as they want. If they decide to only let five-minute-milers in, the number of entrants would go down, but the number of spectators would probably go up.

Truth be known, I'm a loyal Boston spectator, but my hands get kind of sore from clapping forty-five minutes into the first wave. From a spectator's point of view, the smaller the field, the better. I tough it out until the last juggling bandit runs by, but my interest level wanes in proportion to the amount of time elapsed since heartthrob Ryan Hall ran by.

Ryan Hall, by the way, is not a Shirtless Wonder. The Tim Tebow of distance running, Hall has been Tebowing since well before Tebow did. He and his wife, Sarah, also a top marathoner, are Christians, and when they finish a race, they point upward and smile a lot and both seem so cuddly and nice. I've no doubt that if either of them ran past me on the back roads of Hopkinton, they'd wave enthusiastically, and I'd invite them to dinner.

See, just being thin and fast doesn't make a Shirtless Wonder; it's the disdainful attitude. And living here in Hopkinton, a mile from the Boston Marathon starting line, I've been snubbed by the best.

Once, a few days before the marathon, I was chugging along a scenic, two-lane road, dreaming of knee-replacement surgery, when I spotted one of the elite Kenyan runners headed my way.

If you don't follow distance running, you should know that Kenyans rule the sport, all over the world. In 2011, Kenyans won every major-city marathon, and many of the half-marathons and 10Ks, too. So it's the *Boston* Marathon, yes, as won by Kenyans. And we love the Kenyans here in Hopkinton.

Many of the elite runners stay here, and it's a tradition for them to visit the elementary school my kids attended. The day I walked into my son's bedroom and heard him playing the Kenyan national anthem on his recorder was the day I knew I wanted to live here forever.

Two of my kids know the *words* to the Kenyan national anthem—how cool is that?

I say all this just so you know I'm not deranged when I tell you I was out running and I came across a Kenyan. This happens in Hopkinton. Honestly, everyone who runs should move here.

But on this day, the Kenyan marathoner is not really running, just gliding along, just to limber up. My hardest effort is probably akin to his stretching. He's not moving much faster than I am, and he's much more scantily clad, with long elegant legs protruding from silken racing shorts. He, gazelle; I, rhino. No hunter could claim he couldn't tell us apart.

The Kenyan is headed north; I'm going south. We're on opposite sides of the street. Respectful of his privacy, I try not ogle, but as we pass I look over at him eagerly, hoping for eye contact. A nod, maybe. I don't need much, but I'd take it. An autograph? A year of free coaching? A seat on the bleachers at the starting line? We're the same tribe, after all, aren't we?

No. We're not.

No smile, no wave, no nod. He doesn't even look my way.

And they say *my* kind dissociates?

At first, I wondered if it was a cultural thing, like Muslims' disapproval of women running around public streets in shorts and sports bras.

But no, Kenyan women race here, too; there's no shortage of scantily clad Kenyan women runners.

I think maybe it was the horror and shock of a scantily clad, fat American woman who appeared to be slaughtering his sport. That, I can understand. The male ego can be a magnificent thing, but like a garden gnome, it's inherently fragile. If this man felt better about himself by looking down on me, well, I'll just consider it another public service I provide, like picking up empty water bottles on the side of the road.

The marathon, by the way, was two days later. I consulted the newspapers and identified my runner, and I clapped for him when he ran by.

But two hours later, when I got home and turned on the TV to watch the elites finish, I was secretly pleased when "my" Kenyan didn't win. (Go, Karma, go!)

Sometimes people you think are Shirtless Wonders turn out to be nothing like them.

The next year, I welcomed what I thought was a group of Shirtless Wonders to my house.

A dozen elite runners from Greece had come to run Boston and needed a place to stay. My neighbor Bob and I opened our homes to them, and then Bob promptly left the country, leaving me and a few other Hopkinton moms to feed, entertain, and ferry the Greek marathoners around for a week.

Let me be clear: Zeus and Apollo have nothing on these guys. It was as if someone had shaken a copy of *GQ* over my house, and out fell these well-muscled men—alas, not into my bedroom, but my kitchen. But my point is, if anyone has the right to be disdainful and haughty, it would be these beautiful Greek marathoners.

But they were delightful. Only one spoke English well; the other just smiled and nodded. The English speaker invited me to join them anytime they went out for a run.

But, oh, I couldn't.

I was far too busy. I had to pick up kids. I had to clean the paddock. I had a deadline to meet. I had to go buy their olives and assortments of Greek yogurt.

Truth is, of course, I was intimidated. Afraid. Afraid my panting would drown out their relaxed conversation. Afraid they would have to slow down for me. Afraid for them to see my mottled, middle-aged-mom legs in shorts. I consider myself self-actualized but "running with Greek gods" is nowhere in Maslow's hierarchy of needs. I made excuses about why I couldn't go, and when I ran out of excuses I went out and ran alone the other way.

It will go down as one of my life's biggest regrets, somewhere between my divorce and once telling someone Farrah Fawcett was my favorite actress.

The opportunities lost to me because of my fat include going to my high school prom, walking down the beach in a bikini, and getting to sit on the inside of the Super Himalaya ride at the South Carolina State Fair. (You know, the one that spins around at eighty miles an hour and flings everyone in the car to the left, so you have to line up by size, like snapping turtles.)

Also, possibly, marrying George Clooney.

Now my fat—or, more accurately, my exceedingly low self-esteem—has cost me my chance to run with a couple of real-life Greek gods.

I bring this up so you know that *I* know that even Greek gods aren't necessarily Shirtless Wonders. These were sweet and kind men (well, I *think*—hard to say when they're all talking Greek) who played catch with my kids in the yard, and when it was time for them to leave, one gave me an embroidered necklace with a black cross. I wear it every time I run. It connects me in two ways to deities.

It also helps me to remember that true Shirtless Wonders are rare. Often, when I think someone arrogant, the problem is not them, but me. My attitude. My temper. My insecurities. My tendency, born of a childhood too much insulted, to always be watchful of the smallest offense.

Maybe the skinny woman who won't meet my eyes isn't disdainful of me, but self-conscious about her pale legs and non-existent chest. Maybe the shirtless guy won't wave back because he's happily lost in his own head. Endorphins aren't just for fat runners. They're available on demand to skinny people, too. I wear the embroidered black cross to remind me.

And for the thrill of knowing that something a hot Greek guy gave me dangles on my chest.

Meanwhile, it's not lost on me that two of my favorite people not in this world were Shirtless Wonders, so I need to lighten up on their kind. We're different, that's all. They're focused on their heart rates and their muscular tension, and I'm focused on what I can eat later today since I just burned 720 calories on my run.

And we do have something in common, I'm learning. None of us, from fat runners like me to the world's greatest athletes, seem to have a shred of an idea what we're really doing out here. *Why* we're doing what we do.

I'm obsessing about this as Kiawah draws near. With my new and longer workouts, I'm spending twice as much time running as before I started training for this race. And the time spent running before was not insubstantial.

There is pre-workout time (swapping glasses for contacts, searching for iPod, connecting Nike+, picking out clothes that don't make me look fat); then the actual workout (running, pausing to pick wildflowers, pat dogs, and admire sunsets); and then the post-workout time (stretching, showering, and icing my achy parts).

All these things considered, my runs now take a minimum of two hours, and sometimes they stretch to three. And I'm running four times a week. That's a lot of hours. Perhaps my goal is noble, but my methods insane.

Maybe I'd be thinner and healthier if I stopped running altogether. If I took that time and used it to plan healthy meals. Prepared broiled salmon and boiled shrimp and work-of-art salads for dinner. I'd have fewer calluses and wouldn't have to buy nearly so many pairs of shoes.

Why am I doing this to myself? I ask myself when I'm tired. *What is the point? Why do I run?*

A few months ago, I read an interview with Ryan Hall in *Running Times* magazine. Hall, who is one of the top US marathoners, who'd win Boston if they'd only disqualify Kenyans, was asking himself the same questions:

"Something that all runners grapple with, especially elites who are doing it full time is, 'Why am I doing this? What gives it meaning?' because running in itself, it's a fun thing to do, but you don't really produce anything tangible."

If Ryan Hall can't answer these questions, and he *earns his living* running—and running *fast*—how can a single mom like me justify spending so much time and energy on a pastime?

My hero George Sheehan contemplated the question, too. In *Running and Being,* he described soaking in a hot tub and hobbling to bed after a grueling marathon, and overhearing his son asking the rest of the family, "If he's going to feel so bad, why does he do it?"

"Upstairs, I was asking myself the same question," Dr. Sheehan admitted.

The question, I discover, even nagged at my Pre.

"You have to wonder at times what you're doing out there," he said once in an interview.

Imagine that. The greatest distance runner of all time wondering why he ran. This was his conclusion:

"Over the years, I've given myself a thousand reasons to keep running, but it always comes back to where it started. It comes down to self-satisfaction and a sense of achievement."

Not losing weight. Not winning a gold. Self-satisfaction and a sense of achievement.

But here's where we depart, Pre and me. I *don't* have a sense of achievement. And for good reason: Other than being able to run a certain distance without stopping, I don't have any achievements. Not lately, anyway.

I'm long past the thrill of my first few 5Ks and half-marathon. I'm not mentally or physically ready to take on 26.2. I'll never run on Hayward Field or take a victory lap in a T-shirt that says STOP GRAHAM. Not only will I never compete in the summer Olympics, but at my age and weight, I won't even be competitive at my local 5K.

I just run. Slowly. Mile after mile after mile.

In *The Inferno*'s nine levels of hell, Dante made a serious omission: mediocrity. It's worse than avarice and heresy, I think.

The remorseless slayer of potential, mediocrity turns the red embers of enthusiasm to yellow. Everyone's a beginner at first, and early mediocrity is unavoidable, even necessary. But sustained mediocrity advertises something. Laziness, maybe. Or fear.

I remember a discussion from a long-ago philosophy class. The hypothesis was this: If the desire to eat is not accompanied by eating, then the desire is not to eat.

Unless we are physically restrained from an action, the thinking goes, not only are adults free to fulfill our desires, but we're *compelled* to by our human condition. Therefore, if my desire is to be a fast runner or to lose weight, and I don't take the steps necessary to be a fast runner or to lose weight, then I desire something else, no matter what I say.

Maybe I desire mediocrity. It's safe. Comfortable. It doesn't yell at me. But how do you distinguish between deadly mediocrity and a helpful plateau?

The question vexes me, so I lie down until it passes.

Meanwhile, the coaching continues. We work on my breathing. We stretch vigorously. We run backward, and sideways, and around trees. We walk down hills and run back up them. And occasionally, when I can tell Pre needs to laugh, I attempt to do abdominal crunches.

Yeah, you can do more crunches than me, but have you had four C-sections?

One thing: We've had no time to work on my diet. Or maybe we just decide I've suffered enough for one year.

But once he recovered from the initial shock of my caloric in-take—it is, after all, not for the fainthearted—Pre's presence did help me lose a little weight. Imagination, deftly harnessed, is a powerful thing. It's a lot harder to scarf down Pepperidge Farm cookies when you think someone is watching.

Now, don't get excited. I didn't lose a lot, just five pounds. But when my mother met me at the airport for Kiawah, her first words to me were, "You look thin."

twenty-five

The Big 7-0

Seventieth. I came in seventieth.

Not seventieth in the race, which would have been pretty good.

Seventieth in my age group.

Of the 159 women ages forty-five through forty-nine in the Kiawah Half-Marathon, I was solidly in the middle of the pack. I finished in 2 hours, 17 minutes, 20 seconds (but who's counting), clocking an average 10:43 pace.

I may have beaten a thirty-three-year-old, but if I did, she was probably running in a full-body cast.

My mother picked me up at Charleston International Airport, fed me, got me to my rental car, and then returned to Columbia. Like Secretariat, I had to run my race, and I needed to do it alone.

Well, kind of alone.

Race morning dawns, and it's raining. Not drizzling. Raining. It's a steady, cold, dripping rain. This year, there is no eavesdropping on skinny runners waiting in line for the shuttle. Everyone is huddled under their umbrellas and plastic bags, complaining.

I brought three outfits with me. The night before the race, I tried them all on and discarded two. They made me look fat.

This leaves this year's equivalent of ye olde zebra-striped suit: a pink skort and matching, sleeveless V-necked top, which for a year I've been washing four or five times a week. It is faded, but serviceable. To the front, I carefully pin my number, 1193.

When I registered for this race in July, Kiawah had asked for my target pace. Confident in my coach, I'd estimated ten minutes per mile.

This provides a life lesson: If you run with the ten-minute-per-mile crowd, you'll run a ten-minute mile.

Ten forty-three, if it happens to be raining.

Just as in my previous races at Kiawah, I am alone but surrounded by three thousand strangers I know intimately. I speak their language. I know what they've done in their spare time for the past few months. I know most of them ate pasta and bread last night.

I don't mind being alone, except that there's no one to talk to. No one I can talk to, without someone looking at me funny and calling a shrink.

Pelted with rain, we wait for the start. Me, standing still; Pre, antsy, jogging in place. After a moment, I hear him whisper. "I'll give you an easy ten, if you give me a hard three."

Remember Stephanie Saldaña's premise? You know the voices are real when you don't like what they say?

I don't like what I hear. But, as always, I know exactly what he means.

The first ten miles will be easy, at least as easy as they can be for a 154-pound woman whose pre-race meal included a hot fudge sundae (with nuts) from the John's Island McDonald's.

The last three miles will kill me.

"The only good race pace is a suicide pace, and today looks like a good day to die," Prefontaine had said once while he was alive.

Given his eventual end, it was a dumb thing to say, probably one of the many reasons he was so churlish when he first came to me.

Suicide—runicide—does not sound like fun to me, any more than being run over by your own sports car when you're at your physical peak. But when you trust and love your coach, you do what he says without question. Ten easy, three hard. *Que sera, sera*, as my mother used to sing to me. What will be, will be.

The national anthem is sung, the gun is fired, and, after an interminably long wait (two or three minutes), the ten-minute-milers and I start to jog slowly. It takes a minute of jogging just to reach the starting line. Then the 13.1 begins.

Did I mention it was raining? And that I had an especially large mug of coffee that morning?

By the end of the first mile, I'm already sensing a disturbing pressure in my bladder, one I could run through if I'd been on, say, Mile 8. But I'm on Mile 2.

So I do something I've never before done, and duck into a Porta-Potty.

There's no line, so it only takes a moment, but a mid-race stop always seemed to me an act saved for real emergencies. Still, maybe this is one. My shoes are already wet, and my socks soon will be. A soggy bladder, too, seems a bit too much to ask of a body that will be suffering in other ways.

Of course, if I hadn't stopped, I might have come in sixty-ninth, not seventieth. I briefly wonder why they don't hand out catheters with race bibs and timing chips.

Resuming, I feel strong, relieved of a burden both physical and mental. I settle in comfortably behind a man and woman running together. They are both thin, and they are both talking, chatting away as if they're exerting no more effort than it takes to share a couple of lattes alfresco. For three or four miles, I draft them, slogging silently in their wake.

I'm wet and slightly uncomfortable. But like Captain America, I think *I can do this all day.*

"Trust the training," the experts say. No. Trust the coach. I do.

The Kiawah half, a wonderfully flat course, is a much lengthier version of my Syrup Mill Road run: down the road, touch the stop sign, and back again. (Except, of course, there's no touching a stop sign at Kiawah.) The people registered for the full marathon run the same route, only they do it twice.

Any vague dreams I have of running a marathon vanish as I stagger through Mile 9 and see the leading marathoners looping around to run the whole course again.

I'm still not sure I'm going to finish the half.

My socks are soaked, and I feel the rising of two angry blisters. I press on. Mile 10.

As Steve had warned, at this point my energy departs and catches the shuttle bus back to my condominium with its sunken bathtub and still-warm bed. The last three miles are torture, endurable only by the inch.

One more step. Left.

One more step. Right.

One more step. One more step.

More marathoners stream by me, beginning their second loop. *The real runners,* I think in despair. Their energy taunts me.

It was just waste of time. You were right. You've achieved nothing. You're losing five hundred dollars and three vital December days that should be spent decorating and baking cookies. It's selfish to do what you do.

Then the most vicious taunt of all. *You could never run a real marathon.*

What if, instead of finishing in two miles, I had to run this route all over again?

I couldn't. No way. I might be able to make another three or four miles running on fumes, but I wouldn't even make it to Mile 20, which is where they say the wall breaks the steeliest of men. Steve never ran a marathon. And I may very well never be able to, despite twenty years of running, and six months of hard training with a coach of international (and otherworldly) repute.

I don't want it badly enough.

This shames me.

I see people with oval stickers on their cars that say "13.1," signifying that they've run a half. They were selling them at the Kiawah expo.

I'd never put one of those on my Jeep. To me, "13.1" means "Can't Run 26.2."

It's like putting a THELMA'S COLLEGE OF DERMABRASIAN AND VACUUMING on your car where the Harvard alumnae sticker goes. Why advertise mediocrity?

Oh dear God, I'm becoming a Shirtless Wonder.

I look again at the marathoners running past me, and I see that, for many of them, this is still easy. They are running as easily as the eleven-minute-milers were when I left the Porta-Potty and joined them at Mile 2.

Me, I'm hurting. I'm wet, and I'm blistered, and I'm going to finish, yes, I see now, but I hope the cameraman who photographs everyone crossing the line misses my shot.

It occurs to me that the marathoners, too, will hurt in another hour. Many will limp in like me. The marathon demands that even Shirtless Wonders suffer. It's the great leveler of the fat and the thin. It is what it is. We all suffer in the end.

I finish. Not in glory. Not to cheers. There is no one I know at the finish, probably at the whole resort, and even though my name is printed on my bib, I don't hear anyone shout my name. I'm just another runner the road contemptuously spit out.

I gratefully accept a shiny silver cape to warm myself (about two hours and seventeen minutes too late) and a cheap plastic medal, cheap because Kiawah's gone green.

I look for the buffet, but can't find it. I wander, the still-angry blisters continuing to scream. Anywhere else, I'd be lonely and self-conscious in a crowd of this size, but exhaustion tears away your insecurities. I am alone; I'm not sure anyone else is. Everyone seems to have a girlfriend, boyfriend, child, parent, family.

It doesn't matter.

I find the buffet, hobble through the line, and collect a bran muffin and a steaming bowl of bean soup. I don't like bean soup. I wouldn't eat it anywhere but here. But after running for two hours and seventeen minutes in the rain, I would eat warm soupy gravel and pronounce it delicious. The heat soothes me. I sit down, my back against a brick wall, and cross my legs. Then I eat my soup, watching the other spent, hungry people. They look cold, wet, serene. Just like me.

When I finish, I stand and go through the buffet line again to collect a muffin to take back to my condominium. I walk slowly, not because of the blisters, but because something seems amiss. For a reason I can't pinpoint, I am vaguely remorseful.

Then I remember. My cheeks flush with shame.

When I crossed the finish line, I was so engrossed in my blistered feet, and then the hunt for the hot bean soup, that I forgot, completely spaced, my invisible companions.

There were two today, I know. Once strangers, now old friends.

My hero George Sheehan, and my coach, whom I finally remember as I ruefully limp toward the shuttle. I blush for the oversight, for my ingratitude. I'm such a rube.

I didn't even offer them any of my soup.

I board the bus stiffly, duck into the first open row.

"Thank you," I breathe, as I sink into my seat and close my eyes. "Thank you for being here. Thank you for not killing me. Not today."

From another dimension, it's possible to feel grown men beam.

twenty-six

The Lumpy Space Princess in Me

Usually, when my children babble about some TV show they've been watching, I cheerily say, "And *then* what happened?"—feigning interest while wondering what I can make for dinner with twelve carrots and half a box of ziti.

But yesterday, a phrase wafted over the backseat of the car and bopped me hard on the head. It was this: Lumpy Space Princess.

The mental dinner preparations screeched to a stop. I turned around and said to them, "*What* did you just say?"

"The Lumpy Space Princess!" Katherine said, delighted to have my attention. "She's on *Adventure Time!*"

Her brother added, "She's purple, and she's in the shape of a cloud, and she says 'Lumpin!' all the time and makes her mother mad."

Katherine began describing, in intricate detail, what transpired on the last episode, so I went back to planning the ziti. But later, after dinner, I Googled the creature and found out everything I needed to know.

There is, in fact, a Lumpy Space Princess. She herself is not lumpy, but she is the princess of Lumpy Space. She has fangs and a star on her forehead. She has no legs or feet, but she can fly.

Lumpin! It's me! I have my own show and didn't even know!

How else to explain a woman of my shape and size who gets personal training from dead guys in her head?

It's been a little over a week since I returned from Kiawah—moderately sore and decidedly defeated since I'd not achieved anything I'd set out to do.

Seventieth in one's age group is nothing to write home about.

For six months, my goal had been to whip some thirty-three-year-old butt, while, at the same time, whipping my own into shape. Just like I'd been trying to do for the past thirty-three years.

Instead, I seemed to have done nothing more than run in place, just like I always do. Run in place, like a weary rat addicted to his running wheel.

I ran a half-marathon, sure, but I've done that before, and before, at a faster pace.

In four months, I will once again stand on the sidelines of the Boston Marathon, an inglorious spectator hoping someone might do me the honor of handing me her pants.

I'm still divorced, still regret it.

If my mother knew how much time I spent talking to dead guys in my head this year, she'd have me committed and legally adopt my kids.

This is progress? For this, I have bunions? I resolve to throw the green silk dress away. Take it to the Salvation Army. But first, I have to go for a run.

I've been home a week, and have purposely not run since the race. I know rest and recovery is equal in importance to the race and training. But it's time. Today, despite my malaise, I know I have to get back out the door. I dress reluctantly and trudge out.

It is unseasonably warm for New England. We've had very little snow this year, and so although it's nearly Christmas, I'm still running on my usual trails, unencumbered by Yaktrax. This, at least, is good.

I begin my regular run—my old stagnant run before I started training with Steve. Four boring miles through Weston Nurseries, two loops on a dirt road, out and back.

I go out slowly. No Nike+ for me today. Already know the miles; don't want to know the pace. Just a slow, slack jog, like I'm a lithe Kenyan marathoner warming up for Boston.

A mile out, I notice I'm feeling good, perhaps even strong. There's no residual soreness, even though it's been just eight days since Kiawah. My breathing is calm, not labored. In surprise, I think, *I can run faster than this.*

And so I do. I pick up the pace. I'm moving as if it were just an everyday run, not my first day back from a painful half-marathon. This is odd. I've already recovered.

I skip a step and turn my face to the sun. I run a little faster. And then I feel it, something profound. It's unfamiliar, but it resembles joy.

It flickers and darts, like a hawk pursuing a hare.

The feeling starts in my legs, my fairly long legs streaked with varicose veins. Legs dimpled with cellulite, holding up thighs that will forevermore chafe. From there, it scoots past my twelve-pack abs, up my chest, and down bare arms that harden and prickle with goose bumps. But it doesn't stop there.

Like the Kiawah route, it loops around twice. It then scampers across my hair, and tickles my face before darting to center and finally, shyly, contentedly, ducking into my heart.

And there, in its home, I finally recognize it. Happiness. Too long a stranger.

I welcome it back. It's been a very long time.

I have not stopped, and I'm running strong now, sure-footed over pebbled terrain. I reach the point where I usually turn and head for home. But I am not done. We are not done.

In my reverie, I did not notice the celebration. But now I do.

Running with me, on either side, are my faithful companions, a doctor and a rube; soon, I think, to move on to some even happier place.

They are smiling. It is, I realize, our victory lap.

Everyone has their daimons. Both of them, and me. In the end, it doesn't matter if they are real to me, or if I am real to them. "What is truth?" Pilate asked, and still no one knows. My truth is not your truth, and that is the crux of the problem. Did Steve Prefontaine talk to me out there running the flowering back roads of a nursery?

No, no, of course not, no.

Yes. Yes. Yes, of course, he did.

They're always talking, the ones who have left. They're always there in the quiet of our minds. They're just waiting to be summoned.

At the funeral of British author Charles Williams in 1945, Hugo Dyson said, "They go away in order to be with us in a new way, even closer than before." Yes, closer than we think.

"Horatio says 'tis but our fantasy, and will not let belief take hold of him," the doomed Prince Hamlet said.

I let belief take hold, gratefully; therefore, I am not doomed.

I did not, however, win a race. Didn't even come close. Let's be honest: I never will.

But I won something else. Something resembling joy. No, I don't need a ride. I'll never need a ride anywhere again.

Abandoning misery and modesty at the same time, I strip off my shirt, bow to the rapturous sun, and dance into another dimension.

twenty-seven

What I Believe

I believe who I am when I'm running is the closest I'll ever be to my true self.

I believe walking has benefits, but running has more. I believe everyone who can run, should.

I believe there's a lot going on in this world that we don't see.

I believe animals know stuff they're not telling.

I believe our bodies always know what to do next, and if we're stumped, it's because we're not listening.

I believe sweat heals.

I believe atheism is curable, but bunions are forever.

I believe the inability to sit quietly for an hour indicates a deficiency of soul.

I believe ice cream is better for you than celery.

I believe our innermost circle of friends should always include a couple of people who are dead.

I believe ecstasy isn't possible on a full stomach.

I believe insomnia can be cured by exertion.

I believe divorce is always wrong when children are happy and thriving, and there is no addiction or abuse in the marriage.

I believe oxygen is better when inhaled outdoors.

I believe in running.

I believe Pre lives.

epilogue

Ewes Not Fat

In the year 2000, eleven months after my third child was born, I ran the Kiawah Island Half-Marathon. I weighed 180 pounds at the time.

A few days later, still throbbing with post-race endorphins, I started work on an essay about the experience of running as a walrus among gazelles. When it was finished, I sent it to *Newsweek,* hoping it would be chosen for the magazine's "My Turn" feature. It wasn't. When it was rejected, I shopped the piece around to a few other magazines, but found no takers. I then filed it away and forgot about it until 2008, the last year my husband lived in our home.

That summer, I rewrote it, dusting and polishing it lightly. Then, since so much time had passed since my original submission, and since I'd written it with *Newsweek* in mind, I decided to try again. As you know by now, I'm nothing if not persistent, even when the odds aren't so great.

Two weeks after I submitted it, I was driving to our first mediation session when a *Newsweek* editor called and said she'd love to run it and wanted to schedule a photograph the next week. I never told her the magazine had rejected it seven years earlier. The timing of the universe, I've learned not to question.

The essay ran six weeks later, in November 2008, under a headline I wrote: "Confessions of a Fat Runner."

"Aren't you offended by that headline?" some people would later write and ask me.

But others wrote and said they were part of my tribe.

One woman said she'd started running as an excuse to go on race vacations with girlfriends, who are similarly large of girth. They call themselves the Martini Queenies and say they're "last to the finish line, first to the bar." I'm an honorary Queenie now. They sent me a T-shirt.

Others wrote poignantly of their desire to run. Another woman wrote, "I am overweight, but deep inside me there is a runner waiting to cross the finish line. There has not been a woman in my family for at least three generations who has been able to run a mile."

It's been more than three years since that essay ran, and I'm still getting mail about it. One woman wrote recently to say it still hangs on her refrigerator, and she reads it before every race.

It's not that my words were so great, or my experience was so compelling. It's just that we all seek connection with our tribes.

There were, however, some complaints. Some people said I'm not fat enough to get to call myself fat.

This objection showed up not only in my email inbox, but on Internet forums where people posted links to the essay. The trolls had a track-and-field day looking at my photo in *Newsweek,* analyzing my shape, and debating among themselves if I'm worthy to be called fat.

Imagine that. I don't know what's more shocking: that, after thirty years in the South and eighteen years of marriage, I'm divorced in New England with four children and two donkeys. Or that, after a lifetime of torment suffered by this particular descriptive, I find myself enthusiastically defending my right to be fat.

One person who called herself "Kaleidescope Eyes" defended me on Runnersworld.com, saying, "She's not exactly a hard body, but she looks pretty healthy and happy."

I love you, Kaleidescope Eyes, but "Confessions of a Runner with Not Exactly a Hard Body" just doesn't have the same ring.

The quarreling continues. Even my publisher worries I'm not fat enough to have written this book. He fears a James Frey–like scandal will engulf me if I lose any weight. He recommends doughnuts. Finally, after a lifetime of dieting, I've got a bona fide license to eat. But I can only do what my body tells me.

I don't need the doughnuts. I've got the stretch marks. I've got the everlasting awkward, self-conscious gait. I've got the psychological scars.

It's true that, as I write this, I'm the fittest I've been since I got married. I weighed 149 this morning. Thin, for me. I lost five pounds when Glamour Doc put me on Wellbutrin. I went off the pills a few weeks later, but I cling to my new set point like a treasured family heirloom. If ever there's a fire, the first thing I'm saving is these five lost pounds.

I'm hoping they will help me run better, maybe even propel me to train to run a full marathon someday. I hope 149 is my new plateau. Even though I still don't fit in the twenty-year-old, green silk dress, I think I can be happy here.

My teenage daughter says the dress is out of date and ugly, anyway.

Fat is relative. Obesity is not. The medical community has standards for this.

You're overweight if your body-mass index—your weight in proportion to your height—is twenty-five to thirty. You're obese if your

BMI tops thirty.

But as any anorexic can tell you, anyone can be fat. In our own eyes, or in others'.

My current weight—which I maintain only because I'm now running about eighteen miles per week—might not qualify me as fat if I'm standing in line at the Walmart in Bluefield, West Virginia.

It does, however, when I'm standing in line at the start of the Harvard Pilgrim Independence Day 10K.

We can sit around all evening, swilling milk shakes and debating if I'm fat compared with other unemployed southern mothers of four. Not open to debate, however, is if I'm a fat *runner*. Despite the miles I've accumulated over the past twenty years, I remain as out of place at a gathering of runners as a lizard in a litter of kittens.

Yes, I have confidence in my fatness, and I take very seriously all charges that I'm not fat enough to call myself fat. Just not seriously enough to post pictures of my abdomen on the Internet as proof.

For that, just search for "runner" on istockphoto.com. You'll not find my picture there. Nor anyone who looks like me.

Over the past few weeks, we've been looking for a cover image for this book, and it's been freshly obvious how untypical my shape is among runners. Among images of runners, the photographs and illustrations are overwhelmingly of people who are thin.

At one point, my friend Debra-Lynn Hook, who is a photographer as well as a syndicated columnist, spent a few days with me, and we tried getting a photograph of me on the run. Nothing came out of that but a lot of good laughs. The photos I liked, she thought I looked too thin. The photos she liked, I thought made me look too fat.

Always, too fat.

At five foot five and 149 pounds, my calves are muscular and rounded, but when I run, my upper arms flap like a wind sock. In profile, my scarred and doughy abdomen looks like that of a thin woman five or six months pregnant. My thighs still lasciviously touch. Soft mounds of back fat push their way out of the straps of my sports bras. Even now, after all this, there are days I stand in front of the full-length mirror, and I am embarrassed.

I despair of being this shape my whole life.

And, a new development: I also despair of what my body will look like if I were to lose weight.

I'm told wrinkles are more pronounced, the thinner you are, and I'm already a candidate for international Botox aid. When I was younger, I tanned constantly, believing fat is prettier when it's brown. I still believe that. I fear melanoma, yet I still sneak two hours in direct sun like other people sneak cigarettes. As much as I long to be thin, if the choice is fat or wrinkled, I think I'll choose fat.

Then there's my unnerving, growing resemblance to the saggy, baggy elephant.

Because my weight has gone up and down so many times, my skin hangs loosely in places. I still run in shorts, but I know there are people who wouldn't if they looked like me. I see it on their faces as they drive by.

There are folds above my knees, deep horizontal lines that are not pretty, and I suspect they will worsen if I lose another five pounds.

I've been fat for so long that I worry losing weight now wouldn't do me any good. Back and forth, the scale and the refrigerator volley a bitter irony: If I lose weight now, I might actually look worse. I am approaching an age—maybe I've already passed it—at which a little padding improves the package. And no matter how old a woman gets, she still wants to be pretty. My grandmother recently slipped and broke her pelvis. She insisted on applying lipstick and blush before she'd get in the ambulance.

That'll be me. Only, I hope I'll also be yelling to my great-grandchildren, "Be sure to put my running shoes in my bag."

Time goes on. Wrinkles incur. Still, I run.

About a year ago, I made a new friend: the best kind, the kind who sends you whiskey-pecan ice cream, packed in dry ice, on your birthday.

Her name is Jennifer Graham, too. Jennifer Phillips Graham lives in Ohio, and she's a writer like me. (She also has four children, making us practically interchangeable. I plan to send her my next American Express bill.)

Jennifer Phillips Graham told me this story.

She was at a writer's conference and got on an elevator with another woman. They made small talk and exchanged names, and the other woman, another wonderful writer named Eileen Button, said, "Are you Jennifer Graham the runner?"

Eileen, it turned out, had read "Confessions of a Fat Runner" in *Newsweek* and we'd exchanged a few emails, so she remembered my name. She was disappointed when Jennifer Phillips Graham told her, no, that wasn't her.

But imagine that. For me, with sincere apologies to the Bible, this could be the greatest story ever told.

Not Jennifer Graham, the overgrown tomato with a sunburn. Not Jennifer Graham, The Warden. Jennifer Graham, the Runner. And she meant *me.* I could have died happy that day.

At its core, Pre said, running gave him a sense of achievement. Here, all these years, I've been thinking I haven't achieved anything because I haven't lost any weight, but there it is. A sense of achievement that didn't come from my children, or my writing, or my oft-admired ability to remember birthdays. A sense of achievement that comes from the simple fact that I run.

It must have been there all along.

Why then does this seem like an achievement? Any neurologically typical two-year-old can run. Maybe it's because so few of us do it when we grow up. Everyone *can* do it, but not everyone does, because it's hard. Hard to get yourself out the door. Hard to push yourself until it hurts.

I wish it were easier. I wish I were thinner. I wish I looked more like my tribe.

I wish I could run around a lake.

But I did. Didn't I tell you?

It didn't happen the month I started running, or even the next year. I started running, and then we started moving, and by the time I could run three and a half miles without stopping, I didn't live in Columbia. But eventually, we move back.

And one day, I go to my grandmother's house, and I ask her to watch the children. I put on my royal-blue running shorts and my YEAH, BUT T-shirt, and strap on my white-trash armband and iPod, and I walk down her driveway, and then I run around Lake Katherine.

The snapping turtles are still there, lined up on the rocks like ellipses, and there are still the cold creeks feeding the lake, and there's the small peninsula where my mother and I used to picnic.

I run past them, past a smattering of new McMansions, over a dead snake lying on the curb. Past my old piano teacher's house, around to the south side of the lake, where at sunset you can hear the soldiers play taps at Fort Jackson. Past people mowing their lawns, children riding their bikes, a brown-suited UPS man making a delivery. Up a hard hill near the street where the late poet James Dickey lived.

It is a small lake, but so huge when you're panting around it on foot.

I don't stop.

Here, I used to trick-or-treat. Here, I rode my bike. Here, I sold Girl Scout cookies.

The snapping turtles, they ignore me. But with the keen senses of a well-exercised body, I intuit their interest, and their awe. *How can something so big, so clunky, be so fast? Like the hare, she runs!*

Speed is relative.

I run around the lake without stopping. All the way to my grandmother's house. A few years ago, this would have been momentous. Today, it's just another day in the life. My kids are playing with soldiers on the floor of the den when I arrive. No applause. None needed. It's just Mom coming back from her run.

I remember this now and think, of course, this is exactly how it should have happened. No one need cheer. The sense of accomplishment is always within.

I remember something else. A greeting card, with sheep. *Ewes not fat; ewes just fluffy.*

Actually, ewe are fat, I think to myself. *But ewe can run around a lake. And ewe float most excellently high in water.*

When the Zombie Apocalypse comes, and there's no food left on Earth, I'll find my tribe. We'll be the last ones standing. Our fat stores will see us through. We'll strut through the ruins, clean up the mess, kill the zombies, and reclaim the planet. We will do all this, fat.

Fluffy is highly overrated.

Postscript

Back up to 155 today.

But that whisky-pecan ice cream was worth every pound.

Acknowledgments

After *Newsweek* magazine published my essay "Confessions of a Fat Runner," I received an email from Thom Rutledge, a psychotherapist and writer in Tennessee, who said he was "strangely compelled" to tell me that "Confessions" would be the title of my first book.

I feel strangely compelled to thank him. Without the friendly nudge of a stranger, this book might be about heavily soiled laundry, since the first rule of writing is "Write what you know."

After Thom, I must thank the editors and magazines that first published some of these words in essay form: *Newsweek,* of course; Kathryn Jean Lopez and *National Review Online;* Beth Roehrig, Louise Sloan, and *Ladies' Home Journal;* and Katie Neitz and *Runner's World.*

The Boston Globe took a chance on me in 1999, when I'd not yet even visited Boston and couldn't pronounce Faneuil Hall, and continues to publish my essays despite frequent outbreaks of freshly enraged trolls. Thank you to Dante Ramos, Marjorie Pritchard, and Peter S. Canellos, and everyone else who has ever run interference for me, as well as the talented artists who so cleverly illustrate my words. Mark Shimabukuro, now in Tennessee, has been a tireless advocate, a wise editor and a good friend.

Dana Newman, my agent, ignored my willful lack of platform and understood this story even though she's happily married and enviably thin.

Garth Battista, my publisher: Do you have any idea how much it means for a *sports* publishing house to put out this book? I must be an athlete, or something. Thank you, thank you, thank you. May a rising tide lift all boats.

Laura Jorstad, thank you for dotting all I's and crossing all T's and for being a smart and polished copy editor that even an OCD do-it-yourselfer can respect.

My parents, Sally and Jonas Mullen, love me when I'm unlovable, and never once asked to see the manuscript in advance. (My mother says she'll tell her friends it's fiction if anything bothers her. I'm good with that.) I love you both so much, and I'm sorry about the title, but who am I to argue with divine revelation?

My apparently immortal grandmother, Mary Louise Gunn, still lives by Lake Katherine, and even though she thinks running is bad for you, she still watches the kids so I can run around the lake when I visit. Thank you, Gram; I love you, and it's never too late to start running.

My very best friend in the world, Diane Lore, walked the Cooper River Bridge Run once with me. It pained her greatly. She doesn't get the running thing, but she always gets me. Diane—my sister, my self—thank you for being there on the best and worst days of my life. And for all the crazy stuff in between. I love you forever.

My dear friend Debra-Lynn Hook has given me the joy and privilege of editing her syndicated parenting column for the past twenty years. (Check it out at www.debralynnhook.com.) She took a weekend from her crazy busy life to photograph me for the book cover; alas, it turns out, gingerbread men have more aesthetic appeal than doughy, middle-aged women. Who knew?

Thank you, Colella's Supermarket in Hopkinton, for making those wonderful gingerbread runners when the Boston Marathon comes to town. Meghan McCall designed the cookie, and Colleen Chick created art with a tube of frosting. My daughter Katherine thought of using one for the cover, and the lovely and talented Jennifer

MacNeil, www.jennifermacneilphotography, is the genius who thought to position one on a track at sunrise.

Thank you, Weston Nurseries, for letting me run through your beautiful dirt roads and flowering fields. Thank you, Weston Nurseries' employees, for never laughing (at least not to my face).

Nancy Perry: You are an angel, and so beautiful inside and out. Thank you for the firewood, and the zucchini bread, and the heavenly soap, and for giving me the idea of the redneck fence. Thank you for loving Jo-Jo and Foggy even now.

Sue Amendola: Thank you so much for keeping me in the saddle, and for helping me recover from the evil, crazed killing machine that was Dante.

Alberto Salazar: I really didn't have time for you, anyway. But I wish you and Galen Rupp all the best.

Teachers matter. Catherine Lempesis picked me to be a team leader in PE at Dent Junior High in the thick of my overgrown-tomato days. I couldn't believe it and never forgot it. Dr. Henry Price taught me to edit at the University of South Carolina, and no graduate degree will ever make me prouder than that "A."

Father John Murray gets my spiritual back and is a much-appreciated sounding board. Anne Pouch waits patiently for my dinghy to come in, so I can pay her the millions owed for her wonderful web work. I am so grateful for both of you.

Kisses, hugs, and spilled-over gratitude to the rest of my circle of love: Ward and Ingrid DeHaro, Christen Hall, Carol Farrington, Vicky Kessel, Jacqueline Ventura, and Laura Sims. Please be careful. You're turning me into a people person.

Jennifer Phillips Graham: You look beautiful today. I was just kidding about the domain name; you can have it, so great is my love.

And, finally, to my children: I love you more, no matter what. (But I really, *really* wish you would run.)

Photo by Debra-Lynn Hook

About the author

Jennifer Graham was a full-time newspaper journalist until excessive procreation demanded a freelance career. She now writes regularly for *The Boston Globe* and other newspapers and magazines. Graham runs in the suburbs of Boston, where she lives with her four children, two donkeys, two cats, and a border collie. She's still waiting for her farm to come in.